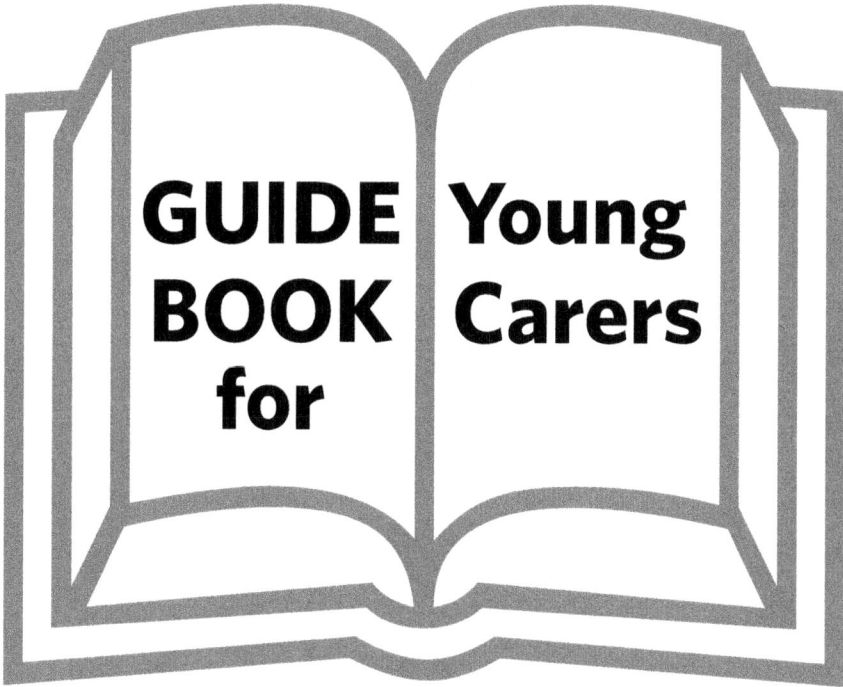

GUIDE BOOK for Young Carers

Mike Raynor

Grosvenor House
Publishing Limited

This book is published by
Grosvenor House Publishing Ltd
Link House
140 The Broadway, Tolworth, Surrey, Kt6 7Ht.
www.grosvenorhousepublishing.co.uk

A CIP record for this book
is available from the British Library

ISBN 978-1-78623-042-3

GOLDEN RULES FOR YOUNG CARERS

A young carer is someone under 18 who provides or intends to provide care for another person. The concept of care includes practical or emotional support.

When I was a child, I was a young carer. Based on my experiences, I have created what I believe is a realistic set of Golden Rules. It has taken me years to realise these. If I could go back in time, this is what I would say to a younger me:

- You should not feel that you have to provide care because no one else is willing to help.
- If you decide to be a young carer, remember it is not your responsibility to provide all the care.
- You should receive support from various people, including family, friends, and health and social care professionals.
- You should be able to choose which caring activities you undertake and which you don't.
- If you are not getting support, then you should ask for it. It's not weak to ask for help.
- It's not selfish to say no. It's also not selfish to say what you need or want.
- Some people will never understand your situation, however hard you try to explain.
- Don't accept everything that adults say. Some adults lie, cheat, avoid problems, ignore the truth and only think about themselves. These will often be the people telling you it is your responsibility to provide care.
- Identify good friends, keep them close, and tell them about your caring role. It will help to chat about your problems with people you trust.
- Don't sacrifice your life to become a carer. Form relationships, pursue an education, gain qualifications and skills, and achieve your ambitions.

ACKNOWLEDGEMENTS

I would like to thank the following people for reviewing various drafts of this book: Helen, Karen, Struan, Graeme, Liz, Sheila and Cris. This book has evolved considerably whilst I wrote it and I am extremely grateful to the reviewers for their feedback.

I would also like to thank the friends who have offered help and support at various times in my life. Some of them are named in this book and some are not. I am humbled by the kindness and compassion I have received. Thanks also to Sharon Rodden, counsellor and psychotherapist, who provided invaluable counselling across many difficult areas.

I would particularly like to thank my wife Helen for all the love, encouragement and patience she has shown whilst putting up with me! In 2015 our daughter Beth was born, and she is a continual source of joy.

CONTENTS

INTRODUCTION

I had a difficult childhood, with my mum being severely mentally unwell and my dad killing himself when I was 12 years old. After Dad's suicide, I was left to look after my mum without any help from relatives or healthcare professionals. I provided continual care throughout the remainder of my childhood, which was awful at times. Rather than choose to do this, I felt I had no other options. I was one of many children in the UK performing difficult caring tasks.

Why I Wrote This Book

I wrote this book because I would like to help present day young carers. Bearing in mind how difficult I found being a young carer, I would like to pass on practical advice based on my own experiences. Therefore I wrote this book and created the website www.youngcarer.info to provide realistic advice to anyone who is experiencing similar challenges to those I encountered.

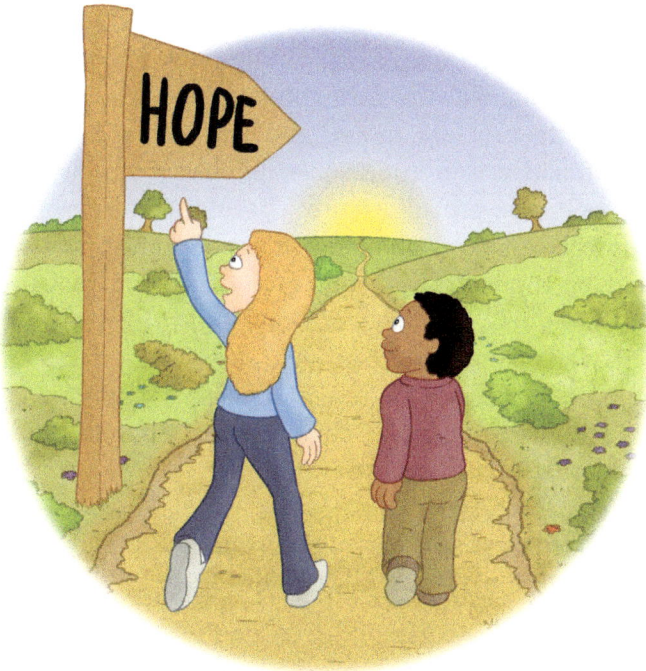

I also want to excite and inspire young carers about the future. When I was a young carer I experienced a range of emotions, including sadness, despair, frustration and anger. At certain times in my adult life I have also felt these emotions. Nevertheless, I have been able to achieve many of my ambitions. I would like young carers to understand there is hope and that they can follow their dreams and live a great life.

Finally, I want to prepare young carers to win against the idiots they will unfortunately encounter in life. The biggest challenge I faced was some of the adults I had to deal with.

An Unknown Number of Young Carers

The data regarding the number of young carers in the UK is very poor. The UK Census 2011 said there were over 177,000 children in England and Wales performing caring tasks. However, research conducted by the BBC in 2010 suggests there could be 700,000 young carers in the UK. This figure could also be inaccurate because some organisations believe that many young carers are not known about, and therefore the actual number could be much higher.

The personal circumstances of different young carers vary significantly. Some will be caring for someone with a physical problem, a mental problem, or perhaps both. Some young carers are known about and are in supportive families, possibly with other family members also providing care. These are given love, kindness, encouragement and practical help. Others are not known about and may receive no support. Some may even have been deliberately left to cope in extremely difficult situations and may receive criticism from others who do not want to provide care.

Being a young carer can have a significant impact on a child's health, happiness, emotional development and performance at school. Some research shows that:

- A quarter of young carers said they were bullied at school because of their caring role (Carers Trust, 2013).

- Young carers are more likely than the national average not to be in education, employment or training (NEET) between 16 and 19 (The Children's Society, 2013).
- Young carers achieve much lower GCSE exam results than average, the difference between nine Bs and nine Cs (The Children's Society, 2013).

There is even less research regarding the emotional impact that being a young carer has on a child. Whilst no statistics are available, it appears clear that young carers often feel sad, lonely, abandoned, frustrated and angry. That was certainly my experience.

How to Use This Book

The book has two parts: Chapters 1 to 4 tell my story and Chapters 5 to 10 give advice for young carers. I am fully aware of the pressures that are placed upon young carers, so I have broken this book into clearly labelled chapters to make information easy to find. The chapters do not have to be read in order. Depending on what is happening in a young carer's life, and how they feel at any particular moment, they may choose to go straight to a certain chapter.

Here is a summary of the chapters covering my story:

Chap.	Title	Summary of Contents
1	Early Years	My childhood and the events that happened before I became a young carer.
2	My Experiences Of Being A Young Carer	My experiences of being a young carer, including how I felt at the time.
3	My Adult Life	My adult life, covering both work experiences and providing care as an adult.
4	The Truth Is Uncovered	The results of an investigation into my childhood and what I believe some family members did and did not do.

and a summary of the chapters providing advice:

Chap.	Title	Summary of Contents
5	Lessons From My Experiences	A review of my experiences as a young carer and some key observations.
6	Advice on Certain Topics	Advice I would give to all young carers about how to cope with their caring role and still achieve their goals.
7	Know Your Rights	A summary of the laws introduced in 2014 that apply to young carers.
8	Tell Your Story	A chapter for young carers to complete to tell their story.
9	Getting Support	Details of people and organisations which offer help to young carers.
10	Conclusion	A brief conclusion.

Some readers may choose to read the entire book. Some may not read my story and instead concentrate on the sections that offer advice. Others may feel they are in a desperate situation and need immediate help, so may go straight to Chapter Nine – Getting Support. There is no right and wrong way to use this book; each reader needs to decide what is best for them. I would, though, encourage all young carers to read The Golden Rules at the start of the book.

Difficult Topics

I should warn readers that in this book I describe some difficult experiences. Using present day definitions, these include child neglect, emotional abuse and physical abuse. I hope that the seriousness of my situation will highlight some key lessons.

My Opinions

I should also point out that I don't have any formal qualifications in child care, so the opinions and advice I give in this book are entirely based on my own experiences. These include my time as a young carer, an adult carer, and in various jobs.

I don't claim to know all the answers, but I do believe others can learn from my successes and mistakes. I've made both in equal amounts. I have experienced a range of emotions, which has been evident from my behaviour at different times in my life. I am not an angel and equally not a bad guy, just someone trying to do his best.

I also want to make it absolutely clear that I do not want or expect sympathy for the experiences described in this book. In many ways I have been very fortunate, and my life could have been much tougher. I know some readers will have had, or might still be having, far more difficult experiences than mine.

Potential Other Readers

As well as young carers, this book may also be of interest to others, including:

- Adult carers.
- Adults who have been young carers in the past.
- Children who have experienced neglect or traumatic childhoods.
- Children who live with a mentally ill parent.
- Children and adults who have experienced a family member's suicide.
- Adults who have a mentally ill family member.
- Medical and health care professionals.

Message to Young Carers

If you are a young carer and you have read this far, I hope you are prepared to go a bit further. I have tried to keep this book brief and to the point. If you don't want to read it, fair enough, it's your choice. Never forget that ... it's your choice.

CHAPTER ONE
My Early Years

My Early Childhood

I was born in Birkenhead, near Liverpool, on 20th November 1973. My parents were living nearby in an area called the Wirral. My dad had a good job as a regional sales manager and my mum had been a teacher, but had stopped teaching when I was born.

When I was about two my dad gave up his sales job and we moved to the West coast of Scotland, where he took a job as a gardener on a private estate. We lived in a place called Ardmaddy for a couple of years and then moved to Achnacloich, both tiny places outside Oban.

I do not remember Ardmaddy, but I remember Achnacloich very well. In our house there was no central heating and we used to have one coal fire in the sitting room. There was no hot running water, and we had to use an immersion heater to heat water. We used to boil kettles for small tasks like daily washes. All the windows were very old, and during the winter the whole house was freezing cold. Sometimes the water supply would freeze, so we would collect ice from a nearby stream and melt it. We used to put lukewarm water down the toilet to make it work, and once a week we would go to the estate owner's house for a bath.

We did not have much money and had to live on a very tight budget. We never had a normal evening meal; I would have something hot like beans or ravioli with bread, Mum would have something similar and Dad would eat sandwiches. Despite having little money, Mum smoked cigarettes. I remember asking Dad about this and he said they helped her nerves.

As I got older I became aware that my parents had a loveless marriage. They slept and ate separately and there was never any physical contact or affection between them. I never saw them hold hands or even kiss. Dad was affectionate and encouraging towards me, but Mum was distant.

Mum's Illness

Throughout my entire life my mother has suffered with serious mental health problems. There were times during my childhood when Mum's illness was not too bad and she would just be very quiet. But when her illness was at its worst I can remember her talking to herself, shouting, laughing for no reason, and her mood changing very quickly. Sometimes she would be rude or aggressive. She took pills every day and regularly went to see a doctor in a nearby village. Therefore I knew Mum was unwell, but I didn't know what was wrong.

I can remember that Mum would often read me a bedtime story, but when she was very unwell she would sit next to my bed talking to herself. At those times I would pretend to be asleep and hope that she would leave my bedroom.

There were times when Mum would become violent and my dad would have to restrain her. I never saw Dad use violence against her. The worst incident I saw was when I was approximately eight years old and I witnessed Mum trying to hit Dad, then kick him and spit in his face. He responded by holding her arms and pushing her out of the room. He got her outside the room and shut the door, and then Mum hammered on the door for a while.

No one in Mum or Dad's families ever spoke about Mum's illness. She could be in the room and very unwell but people would carry on chatting as though nothing was wrong. Therefore I assumed that we should never discuss her illness.

I can remember worrying a lot about it, wishing that I had a normal mum, like other people.

Memories of Dad

I can remember Dad being very hard-working and trying his best to look after Mum. He was very cheerful with me and we used to collect firewood, go for long walks in the countryside and work together on the estate.

Dad was very keen on values and he used to explain to me what was right and what was wrong. He was also adamant that people should stand up for themselves. I was bullied at primary school, so Dad made me a punchbag out of old clothes and taught me how to throw punches. I then hurt the bully and got in trouble with the teachers, but Dad gave me extra pocket money.

When I was about ten, I can remember a friend of Dad's called Bob coming to visit. Bob had worked with Dad as a salesman, and had stayed in the company and become a senior manager. Bob offered Dad a very good job, but Dad declined. I remember Bob trying to persuade him to change his mind, but Dad continued to refuse. Later in this book I describe why I think Dad declined this job.

At times Dad was a bit of a risk-taker. Sometimes our car had no insurance because we couldn't afford it, and Dad simply hoped that the police would not stop us. When cars were no longer roadworthy he used to rally them around the local fields and then sell them for scrap.

I can remember thinking that Dad didn't like Mum's family. He would be polite to their faces, but would spend a lot of time out of the house when they visited. My mum's sister used to send letters and cards with long-winded messages of love, even though she never helped in any way. My dad would take these letters and cards into the bathroom and repeatedly read out the messages and then flush the toilet. He used to laugh every time he did this.

In the months before his death I can remember Dad being very sad. He had low self-esteem, said he was worthless and that he was a failure. In retrospect, I believe he had chronic depression. I also believe he felt exploited by Mum's family. I remember feeling very sad that Dad was so unhappy, and also thinking that he was not a failure in my eyes.

Dad's Goodbye and The Journey South

One Sunday, when I was twelve years old, the day started out like most other days. Dad and I spent some time together collecting firewood whilst Mum was doing housework. However, later in the day Mum and Dad had a big argument, and Dad decided that they would separate. Dad said he would stay in Scotland, and Mum and I would travel to her parents in Widnes. At first Mum would not accept this, but then Dad packed her and my bags. He was not angry as he did this; he just calmly packed what we needed to travel to Mum's parents.

There was an evening bus that travelled from Oban to Glasgow and it passed near our house, so the plan was Mum and I would catch the bus to Glasgow and then get a train to Widnes. When it came time to leave the house, Dad held out his hand to shake mine. I shook his hand and saw the tears in his eyes. I reached my head up to give him a kiss and he kissed my cheek as I kissed him.

Mum and I went outside and stood waiting for the bus. I could see Dad in the house, in floods of tears as he watched us. He then came outside the house sobbing, holding a handkerchief to his face because he was crying so much. He shouted, "Goodbye, Michael, I love you," and then went back into the house. I think even then I knew something was wrong in the way he said goodbye.

The bus arrived shortly after this, and Mum and I left for Glasgow. I can remember sitting on the bus not knowing if I would see Dad again. I also thought about other parts of my life, such as not having had the chance to say goodbye to my schoolfriends, and wondering where I would go to school and if I would enjoy it. Every part of my life seemed to have been ripped apart, on what had started as an ordinary day.

When Mum and I got to Glasgow we had missed the last train to England, and we did not have enough money for a hotel, so we spent the night in Glasgow Central Station. At night the station had a lot of homeless people and alcoholics sleeping there, and I can remember being scared. Mum fell asleep in a chair, so I stayed awake and watched our bags. Two alcoholics sat near us, so I moved our bags closer to me. One said in a soothing voice, "Don't worry, I would not steal from a little lamb like you."

In the morning we caught the first train to continue our journey to Widnes. I did not know it at the time, but Dad was already dead.

As we were on the train close to Widnes, my mum, who was really unwell and speaking to her voice a lot, pooed herself. I didn't know until we stood up to get off the train, and I can remember other passengers laughing. I could not believe people were laughing when we were in such an awful situation. I can remember feeling both embarrassed and very angry.

Dad's Death

We arrived at my Mum's parents and they criticised Dad for separating from Mum. The next morning, whilst I was eating cornflakes, they told me the police had been during the night and said that Dad had died. My grandparents then drove Mum and me back to Scotland.

When we were back in Achnacloich a policeman visited and read me a letter that Dad had written before he died. It said he loved us and he was sorry. After reading it the policeman said, "That is the most difficult thing I have ever had to do."

Mum kept saying that Dad was still alive and he must be at work. My grandparents then left to drive to a shop in Connel to get some food, so I was by myself in the house with Mum.

In the living room, a seat cover had been taken off an armchair, and it was folded up and on top of a sideboard. I picked up the seat cover and opened it. It was covered in a huge bloodstain. I knew I was staring at my dad's blood. I spoke to Mum about it and showed her the seat cover. She then burst into tears. I went upstairs and sat on the end of my bed, feeling numb. Even though I was twelve years old I didn't cry or get upset, I simply sat there, knowing that tough times were ahead. After a while I came downstairs and realised that Mum had started a bonfire in the garden. She had dragged the armchair outside and set fire to it.

How Dad Died

As an estate gardener, one of my Dad's tasks was shooting rabbits that were damaging crops. For this he had two shotguns.

After Mum and I had caught the bus to Glasgow, my dad had tidied our house, walked to his work and collected a shotgun from his gun cabinet. He came home, pointed the gun at his chest and shot himself. His body was found in the armchair the next day by a neighbour when he did not arrive for work. I hope he died instantly and did not feel any pain.

Returning to School

I returned to school three days after Dad's death. I think my main reason for going back so quickly was that I did not want to be in the house with my mum and grandparents.

After Dad's Death

My dad's funeral took place at a crematorium outside Glasgow. At the reception afterwards, my grandfather (Mum's father) said to me, "Your father has taken the easy way out. You are now the man of the house, so it's now your responsibility to look after your mother." I remember thinking this was a dreadful comment for a grandfather to make to his twelve-year-old grandson under any circumstances, but to do so at my father's funeral was even worse. I felt that he did not want to take any responsibility for helping with Mum and had not shown any consideration for my feelings at my dad's funeral. I can remember feeling both sad and angry.

The house we lived in came with the gardener's job, so we had to move. My dad's employer, Mrs Jane Nelson, was a very kind woman and she allowed us to stay in the gardener's cottage for several months until we found a house. The choices were moving to England to be close to family, or stay on the West coast of Scotland.

The Move to Bonawe

My grandfather arranged for a council house in Bonawe, a tiny hamlet 15 miles outside Oban. My grandparents stayed with us until after the move, but continuously complained and blamed my dad for the situation. Whilst I was disappointed and angry with my grandparents' comments, it is worth mentioning that they did stay with us during this time. No one from Dad's family came to help with the funeral or the move. Shortly after the move, my grandparents returned to England. For the next five years I rarely saw any relatives.

CHAPTER TWO
My Experiences of Being A Young Carer

I was a young carer for five years, between the ages of 12 and 17. As an only child with a very unwell parent, I did not feel I had a choice other than to do this.

My Time As A Young Carer

Of my parents, my dad was dead and my mum was seriously mentally unwell. Mum's mental illness generally followed a pattern of six weeks of reduced illness, followed by two weeks of intense illness.

One of the main aspects of her mental illness was that she heard a voice in her head. She thought this was someone communicating to her, so she would respond, even though there was no one there. I used to watch my mother as she would speak with, and sometimes shout at, empty chairs and empty corners of rooms. Sometimes she would burst out laughing, whilst at other times she would start crying. Her mood towards me would change very rapidly, and in a short period of time she could demonstrate a range of pleasant and very unpleasant emotions. As a child, I found it upsetting and scary to be in a house with someone who was so mentally unwell.

Even when her illness was not too bad, she was unable to show any sort of affection, love, encouragement, guidance or emotional support. It did not feel that I was living with a parent; instead I felt as if I was in a house with a very unwell adult that I was responsible for. I felt completely alone.

I hardly ever saw any of Mum or Dad's families. I had weekly phone contact with my grandmother (Dad's mother) and relatives visited very occasionally.

We lived in a two-bedroom council house in a very small village called Bonawe, in a remote location, 15 miles outside Oban in Argyll. Bonawe was very isolated and there were no village facilities or shops. The house did not have central heating and instead there was a fireplace in the sitting room. When we first moved into the house we were told by the Council that the fireplace should not be used because there had previously been a chimney fire. Therefore we used a small electric heater to heat the sitting room, but no other rooms were heated. A couple of years later we were told the fireplace could be used, so I used to collect firewood and sometimes we would buy coal. Even if we lit a fire in the sitting room, all the other rooms remained unheated.

None of the windows in the house were double glazed, they were single-glazed windows with wooden frames. Even when they were shut there were still draughts, and during winter the house was freezing cold. We only had hot water if we turned on an immersion heater for two hours, so I used to have two baths per week. Daily we used to boil kettles to have a wash.

We did not have a washing machine, so we hand-washed all our laundry. Sometimes that was done by Mum, but when she was unwell I would have to do it. We didn't have a phone because we could not afford one. There was a phone box in our little village, so we could make phone calls from there, but we could not receive calls.

We had very little money because my mum did not work and we relied on social security benefits. During all my time as a child carer I managed the family finances, so I monitored our bank accounts, ensuring that bills got paid and that there was enough money for basic needs.

My mum was on pills and I had to supervise her medication. I did not know what the pills were, but the instructions on the boxes said how regularly they should be taken. Sometimes when Mum was unwell she would forget to take her pills, so I would have to prompt her.

At home we ate very basic food. With such little money and no car, we only bought food that we could carry in shopping bags on the bus. We bought bread, milk, cereal, some fruit, biscuits, and tinned foods like baked beans, ravioli and spaghetti. My usual breakfast was a bowl of cereal, and dinner was beans, ravioli or spaghetti with three pieces of bread.

At school I initially got free school meals because I was from a low income household. Then the system changed and we received extra social security benefits to pay for my lunches. This meant that I could leave the school at lunchtime and visit the local shops.

Twice a week my mum would travel on the school bus to Oban to get shopping. Sometimes she was unwell and she would speak to the voice she heard, behave erratically and be rude to other passengers. Sometimes I would have to sit next to her to try to calm her down. Mum's behaviour on the bus always made me feel embarrassed and angry.

The neighbours were polite when we saw them, but they made no effort to get to know us. Many of them knew that Mum was mentally unwell because they had seen her behaviour, but nobody ever mentioned it. Mum did not have any friends or a social life.

Generally my social life was at school. There were no boys of my age in the village so I had no friends there, but I had a very good friend who lived seven miles away and sometimes I would cycle to see him. I had another good friend in Oban who I would often stay with, which was always a welcome break from living with Mum.

I set the rules in the house because Mum was not well enough to know what was right and wrong. I had to set rules regarding matters such as how we spent money, what food we bought and what household jobs needed to be done. I decided how I should behave and how I should approach things such as my school work and social life.

Physically Restraining Mum

I cannot remember the first time that Mum tried to hit me, or the first time that I had to restrain her, but it became a regular event during her two-week periods of being very unwell. I had to block blows, hold her arms, block kicks and force her to the floor. When I was doing this she would be shouting and swearing at me. Sometimes I had to use considerable force to control her. Very few people have experience of physically restraining someone who is mentally unwell. My experience is that the ill person does not try to limit their actions, so they use all their strength. Also, they do not feel any pain. Therefore the person restraining them has a considerable challenge.

I have no idea how many times I physically restrained Mum during the five years that I was a young carer. It certainly happened regularly during every two-week period that she was very unwell. Often Mum was bruised after I had restrained her.

I decided not to tell anyone that I was physically restraining Mum. Mum and Dad's families and the local doctor's surgery all knew she was very unwell, that Dad had committed suicide, and that I was a child now living with a mentally-ill adult. No one wanted to discuss Mum's mental health, and as I had been left to deal with her, I was going to handle the problem any way I had to.

I kept my problems a secret and completely separate from school. I liked my friends and teachers a great deal, but I never discussed my mother's illness or my role as a carer. This was because I wanted to lead as normal a school life as possible. I was also concerned that if the authorities thought the situation was serious they might put me into care. I was worried this might result in being moved to a different area, away from friends and school, and might affect my chances of getting to university and finding a good job. ***My biggest regret now is that I didn't tell friends and adults I trusted what was happening.***

Involvement of Dad's Family

I was very close to my dad's mum, who I called Nan. She lived in Heswall in north-west England. Sometimes she would visit Bonawe and sometimes I would travel to visit her, so I used to see her a couple of times a year. I phoned Nan every week from the payphone in our village.

Nan was in her seventies and had arthritis but would travel all day to get to Bonawe. She would catch a bus from her village to Liverpool, get a train to Glasgow, cross Glasgow to another station, catch a train to Oban and then travel out to Bonawe. When she visited, Mum was often very rude to her. When I went to school Nan would have to spend the whole day with my mum, so she used to spend a lot of time in the bedroom to avoid her. I can remember Nan describing me as 'an old head on young shoulders'.

When I was a teenager, Nan told me that Mum had been very unwell when I was a baby, so I had been cared for by some of Dad's family. She did not tell me any details other than Mum's family had refused to help.

My dad's sister and her husband never visited in the five years we lived in Bonawe, even though they knew Mum had serious mental health problems. During those five years we had a handful of visits from other members of Dad's family, so approximately one visit per year. These would be brief visits of a couple of hours that would involve a drink and a polite chat, but then they would leave.

Involvement of Mum's Family

Mum's sister and her husband lived outside Glasgow so were the closest of all our relatives, but they would only visit for an hour, once or twice a year. Mum's parents used to visit once a year, but that stopped when I was about 14.

When I was approximately 14 years old my mum's parents drove to Scotland and spent some time with my aunt and uncle outside Glasgow, and then came to Bonawe. My mother was very unwell when my grandparents arrived, and they repeatedly said to me, 'Your father made your mother unwell.'

One evening, when it was time for dinner, my mother placed a loaf and some jam on the table and said we would have to have sandwiches. My grandparents looked at me in disgust and complained that they needed hot food because they were pensioners.

My grandfather then said, 'We are not putting up with this. We are leaving.' They started packing their stuff and loading their car. He said to me, 'I don't know how you put up with this.'

I replied with, 'I don't think I have much choice.' He looked at his feet and then carried on packing.

When it came time for them to leave, a discussion started about why there was so little food in the house, and I explained we had very little money. My grandfather gave my mother some money and then they left. It never occurred to my grandparents to drive to Oban to buy food, to take us out for a meal or even to buy a takeaway.

My grandparents would have arrived back at my aunt and uncle's house near Glasgow earlier than planned, and I imagine they would have explained why. Needless to say, we did not hear from my aunt or uncle.

Support from Friends

I had a good friend who lived in Oban with his mum and step-dad, Catherine and Tommy. Sometimes they invited me to stay at their house, which meant I could attend social events like school discos and rugby training sessions. It also meant I could go to rugby games that involved travel outside the Bonawe bus times. I never worried about leaving Mum for a night because I thought she could cope by herself for short periods of time, which she had to do anyway when I was at school. Every evening I stayed at my friend's house, Catherine cooked a three-course meal and every morning she cooked a full breakfast. The food was excellent and completely different to what I had at home. Tommy would give me a lift to Bonawe if there were no buses available. They were both extremely kind and generous.

For several years I had a holiday job as a gardener at a stately home near Bonawe called Ardchattan Priory. The gardener and his wife, George and June, lived in the gardener's cottage with their four children, two dogs, a cat and a lot of tropical fish. Their house was never quiet and I liked the life and energy in their home. George used to tell lots of stories from when he had travelled the world in the Merchant Navy. June used to supply lots of tea and biscuits and add to George's stories. There were always jokes being made and I can remember laughing a lot. George and June were also extremely kind and generous.

My Opinion Of My Situation

When I was a young carer I remember sitting on the edge of my bed with my head in my hands.

I can remember summing up my situation as follows:

- My father was dead, having died a miserable, violent death.
- My mother was extremely mentally unwell.
- I was an only child, so I did not have any brothers or sisters.
- My family were not interested and lived a long way away.
- Our doctor knew about my mother's condition but was not interested.

- We lived in a tiny hamlet, miles away from anywhere.
- We lived in a very run-down council house.
- The neighbours knew my mother was unwell, but never mentioned it or made an effort to get to know us.
- We had very little money and relied on social security benefits.

During that time I felt a range of very intense emotions. I felt deserted by my family and a lot of anger towards them for leaving me in this situation. I was extremely frustrated that others could leave/ignore Mum's illness and our situation, whilst I felt I had no choice other than to stay.

I felt lots of emotions when I had to physically restrain Mum. I felt sad, alone and without support. Then I felt even more anger towards my family. I felt guilt and shame that I had bruised Mum, even though I believed I had no choice. I felt completely trapped in a situation I did not want.

I was extremely embarrassed when Mum was mentally unwell in public, for example, on the local bus. I could not believe that people took her behaviour at face value and could not see that she was mentally unwell. This made me even angrier.

I sometimes felt despair and loneliness. These emotions resulted in me experiencing a huge amount of stress. I hid this from friends and family and thought it was a burden that I had to carry alone.

It became obvious to me that no family members or medical professionals were going to help me. My options were to survive or fall apart. I chose to survive. I believed that survival required me to supress my emotions and I became very self-sufficient. I also felt that society had failed me. Therefore I was going to abide by the rules of society that I agreed with, but I was going to ignore those that I disagreed with. I became completely used to separating different parts of my life, telling certain people certain things, and keeping a lot of secrets. At times I was completely unemotional and only saw life in black and white terms. Sometimes, I'm not proud to say, I demonstrated no consideration towards others.

I had been interested in joining the military since I was about ten years old. I wanted to do a job that involved challenge, adventure, working in a team, and where I could improve myself. Following Dad's death and the lack of support from my family, the military appealed even more.

I recognised that I needed qualifications to achieve my ambitions. Therefore I started studying every evening, sitting in my freezing cold bedroom and reading for hours. I also started physically training. I designed a training programme consisting of runs, bike rides, push-ups and sit-ups. I stuck to this regardless of the weather, which meant I often went out running in the rain. Some of the locals stared at me whilst others laughed. I just carried on running.

Staying Away from Relationships With Girls

I noticed girls throughout my time at school and felt very strongly about several in particular. I looked at these girls and some of them looked back. There were a few girls, on average one per year, that I really fancied and I think they liked me. There was a lot of eye contact, little smiles, and even more eye contact.

However, I did not ask any of these girls to be my girlfriend. I worried about things like how would I go on dates when I lived in such a remote place, how much money it would cost and how I would introduce Mum. I stayed away from relationships, which meant I was sacrificing elements of my life to be a carer. I stopped looking at these girls and they stopped looking at me. This meant I stayed single and again isolated.

Physical Effect On Me Of Being A Young Carer

I believe the stress of being a young carer affected my physical health. I started suffering with awful migraine headaches when I was approximately 14 or 15 years old. I didn't get these often, but when I did I felt dreadful. I would be physically sick and have to lie down for hours. I went to the local doctor's surgery about these headaches but was told that some teenagers suffer migraines as they go through puberty. I now know that migraine headaches are sometimes caused by stress.

When I was about 16 I started suffering with fainting. Oddly enough, this only happened when I was at home and never anywhere else. At the time I was extremely fit because I was doing a lot of physical training. Again, I went to the doctor but was told it could be low blood pressure and I might be standing up too quickly. The advice from the doctor was to stand up slowly.

In retrospect, I feel disappointed that my mental, physical and emotional health needs were not better looked after.

Focusing On School and Rugby

I enjoyed school, both the studying and the social life. I made some great friends who I have stayed in touch with all my life. There were many other good friends who I have lost touch with as our lives have gone in different directions. I was also lucky to have some excellent teachers. Overall, I can remember lots of laughter, jokes and farting.

I started playing rugby at school and it became more and more of a focus for me. I loved the physical challenge, the competitiveness and the aggression. Rugby felt like an outlet for all the challenges in my life and it was a way to rid myself of anger. At the time it felt fantastic to be on the rugby pitch, filled with aggression and taking it out on the opposition. I loved winning and I loved beating my opponents, regardless of how it made them feel. What did they have to complain about? They knew nothing of the challenges in my life.

In my second last year at school I was made a prefect and in my final year I was appointed Head Boy. I was probably seen as responsible and reliable. I thought it would look great on my CV and I enjoyed the position of responsibility.

One of my friends had a car and he was generous in giving me lifts, and occasionally he and some others would drive out to visit me. If there was a knock on the door and Mum was unwell, I would tell her to go upstairs before I answered the door. This was to keep the situation hidden from my school friends and try to maintain a normal social life.

Involvement of Doctors

Poo In The Kitchen Sink

Twice when I was 15 or 16 I returned home to find that my mother had smeared her own poo over the kitchen sink. She had pooed into a bucket, emptied her poo into the kitchen sink, mashed it up with her fingers and forced most of it down the plug hole. On both occasions I repeatedly filled our kettle in the bathroom, boiled the water and then poured it all over the sink. On both occasions I phoned the local surgery and a doctor came to visit, but both times they simply asked Mum not to do it again and then left.

Hospital Admission Following Collapse

In 1990 I attended a three-day course with the army. Whilst I was away I was told by an officer that my mother was OK but had been admitted to hospital. She had tried to walk the 15 miles from Oban to Bonawe on a very hot day whilst carrying shopping bags, and had collapsed with exhaustion and heat stroke. She was admitted to hospital for a couple of days, when apparently she demonstrated serious mental health problems, but nothing further happened after her discharge from hospital.

Family Awareness of Bruising

In 1990, in my fifth year as a young carer, my mum's sister visited and spotted that my mother had bruises from where I had been restraining her. I was accused of beating her up and several days later a doctor spoke to me about the bruises. I explained that I had to restrain Mum when she was very unwell. The doctor did nothing other than to suggest that if Mum was being difficult I should stay out of the way.

After the doctor had spoken to me, my mum's sister and her husband came to visit us. My aunt took my mother into the kitchen and my uncle spoke to me. The conversation went like this:

My uncle said, 'You need to stop hitting your mother.'
'I have to defend myself and also try to restrain her!' I replied.
'You are bigger than her now, so I don't believe that,' he said.
I replied with, 'She is seriously mentally unwell and tries to hit me.'
He said accusingly, 'What sort of a son hits his own mother?'
'A son that is defending himself from his mother,' I said.
He raised his voice and said, 'I am telling you that you are wrong.'
I replied with, 'I am telling you that I don't have an alternative.'

The conversation continued like this for quite a while, though my uncle got steadily angrier that I was disagreeing with him. After we had been speaking for a while I gulped, which he saw, and he said:

'You just gulped. You are cracking. You are about to start crying.'
'No I'm not. We have just been talking for a while,' I replied.
'Yes, you are. You are cracking,' he said.
I paused and said, 'Let me make this clear. You are in your mid-forties and I am sixteen, but I have looked you in the eye throughout this conversation, replied to everything that you have said and repeatedly pointed out that you are wrong.'
My uncle paused, smiled at me, and then said, 'You know, Michael, I have got this wrong.'
'Really?' I replied.
'Yes, I had thought you were just a violent thug, but actually you are a cold, calculating, evil boy.'
I immediately felt anger surge throughout my entire body. I paused, took a deep breath and then said, 'I don't see any point in continuing this conversation.' I stood up and left the room before I exploded.

Whilst all I wanted to do was punch him, I knew that being violent would support his argument. About five minutes later my aunt shouted up the stairs that they were leaving. I came downstairs and my uncle was still staring at me. My aunt held out a £5 note and said it was pocket money for me, but I replied by saying that I did not need it because I had a part-time job. My aunt looked really embarrassed, stuck the £5 in my shirt pocket and then quickly left with my uncle.

Dad's family were more supportive, but did nothing of any real help. They said they knew how bad Mum could be and that I would not have bruised her without reason. They made some stupid comments like, "If your mum is being difficult, go for a walk until she calms down," and "Don't get angry; just ignore what she is saying to you." They returned to their lives and I was left with Mum.

What Happened Next

After my family and the local doctor's surgery knew that I was physically restraining Mum, I still made the decision to keep my problems a secret from school. This was because:

- If my family and a doctor thought it was acceptable to leave me with Mum when she was so unwell, why bother telling anyone else?
- I was attending courses with the army and did not want to affect my chances of becoming an army officer.
- I felt that I could cope with the situation until I went to university.

I knew it was not my fault that the problem existed, and I also knew that I had been left to cope in dreadful circumstances whilst all the adults had left. However, when the bruises came to light, I was criticised by those people who had done nothing. I felt even angrier at my family.

When Mum became very unwell again, I again found myself having to restrain her, not because I wanted to, simply because I did not have a choice. Again she was bruised, but because Mum's family and the local doctors never checked how we were doing, they never saw the new bruises.

Finishing School and Leaving Home

Shortly after finishing school in 1991 I was accepted onto a degree course at Dundee University. Whilst I wanted to join the army, I was keen to get a degree because I knew qualifications would help me get a job when I left the army.

My mum and grandfather decided that when I left home, Mum would move to Widnes. My grandfather was moving into a sheltered accommodation flat, which meant that Mum could live in his old house. She was going to move house several days before I started at university, so my grandfather came to Bonawe to take her to Widnes. He repeatedly complained that he should not have to do this and that I should accompany my mother to Widnes. I eventually said, "I start university in three days," to which he replied that there was plenty of time for me to get to Widnes and then get a train to Dundee. I responded with, "I have my own life to lead", after which he walked away.

After my mother and grandfather left, I spent three days in our empty council house. The neighbours lent me a sofa bed and I slept in my dad's old sleeping bag. I spent the days walking and reading, which was really pleasant after life with Mum. My five years of being a young carer had come to an end, which felt like a huge weight being lifted off my shoulders.

June and George kindly offered to take me from Bonawe to Dundee and they took a day off work to do so. Upon arrival in Dundee they insisted on finding my halls of residence, helping carry my bags, walking me to my room, and getting me settled. They then gave me £20, saying, "Enjoy your first night in the student's union."

CHAPTER THREE
My Adult Life

Purpose of This Chapter

It may seem strange that a book on being a young carer contains a chapter called 'My Adult Life'. The main reason I have included this chapter is I want to excite and inspire young carers about what their lives could be. Many young carers feel they are carrying the world on their shoulders and consequently find it difficult to dream about the future. However, I believe it is very important to think about the future.

I want to show young carers that they can fulfil their ambitions. I have been able to achieve my goals whilst continuing to provide some care for my mother. These are some of my achievements:

- Going to university and getting a degree.
- Working abroad in Canada and Israel when I was a student.
- Joining the army, getting promoted and leading teams of soldiers.
- Returning to university and getting a Master's degree.
- Working as a Ceasefire Monitor in dangerous areas of Sudan and Georgia.
- Becoming the security manager of an international company and working in the UK, US and Europe.
- Starting a successful business.

I also want to show that my successes have taken hard work over a long time, and have often required lots of small steps. I have set myself small challenges, kept working hard, adapted to changing situations, dealt with setbacks, and eventually big improvements have happened in my life.

In terms of providing care, I want to explain the problems and successes I have encountered as an adult carer. Many of these have lessons for young carers. Finally, I want to demonstrate that young carers need support in providing care. If young carers try to provide all the care by themselves, it is likely to have a negative effect on their lives.

Attending University, 1991–94

In 1991, just before my 18th birthday, I started a degree at Dundee University. This was the first time in the life that I felt able to enjoy myself without having to worry about Mum. My first year was a massive pressure release which included drunken parties and not much studying.

In my second and third years I partied less and studied more. Twice I went abroad by myself on working holidays. One summer I went to Toronto in Canada and worked as a removal man, and another summer I went to Israel to work on farms called kibbutzim. The flight to Canada was my first flight overseas and only my second time abroad. For me it felt normal to be alone, in an unusual situation and simply having to cope.

At university I often felt confused and frustrated, but I portrayed a different image. I still had a lot of pent-up anger, combined with a lack of experience in emotional relationships. I wanted a girlfriend but was either too shy, inexperienced or drunk to speak to girls. I was disappointed when I encountered people who never tried to see a situation from someone else's point of view. Sometimes my frustration erupted as an angry outburst, but whatever my point, it was lost as the focus was on my outburst.

Whenever I returned home during holidays there were problems with Mum such as loss of weight due to not eating properly (on one occasion her weight decreased to approximately six stone), not washing herself properly, wearing dirty clothes and neglect of financial affairs. It was in the early 1990s that she started drinking alcohol.

Serving in The Army, 1995-2000

I joined the army in 1995 and served for five years. I completed a year of officer training at the Royal Military Academy Sandhurst, after

which I joined The King's Regiment, which was the infantry regiment for Liverpool and Manchester. They have since been amalgamated and are now The Duke of Lancaster's Regiment.

I was initially posted to Cyprus, during which time I did training exercises in Jordan, Egypt and Kuwait. I then did six months in Northern Ireland attached to The Royal Irish Regiment. After that I returned to the King's Regiment in the UK, when I did several short deployments to Northern Ireland and a training exercise in Belize.

Mum's Illness When I Was In The Army

During my five years in the army I phoned home weekly and often knew that Mum was unwell. My grandfather visited her weekly, but provided no actual care or support. Whenever I returned home on leave I always had to manage Mum's finances, clean her house, perform any necessary repairs and stock her cupboards with food.

In 1997 and 1998 some local scumbags noticed that Mum was unwell and burgled her house, stealing some of her and my belongings. I had all the windows replaced to improve security. On another occasion I was on leave and Mum and I were out of the house, but when we came back I found the back door had been broken down. As I went in the back door a burglar ran out of the front door, so I chased him down the street. Fortunately, some workmen were nearby and they jumped on him. I held the burglar until the police arrived, during which time I politely informed him that I was in the army. He did not reply. He was arrested and charged with burglary. These events really upset Mum and were a serious concern for me because it highlighted how vulnerable she was.

In 1999 Mum was sectioned under The Mental Health Act, which means a doctor decided to detain Mum in a psychiatric care unit (a hospital for people suffering with mental illness) for her own good. This was the result of one night when she had left her house in the early hours of the morning wearing her night-clothes and dressing gown, walked three miles to a motorway and lain down on a roundabout. A motorist had phoned the police, who picked her up, after which she saw a doctor and was sectioned. I was stationed in Northern Ireland when this happened and did not mention it to anyone. I was used to coping alone and, besides, I didn't want my work colleagues to know about Mum's mental illness.

Leaving the Army

I enjoyed my time in the army but left in 2000 because I did not want a long-term career. I had been promoted a couple of times and left at the rank of Captain. I met some great people who I will stay friends with for the rest of my life.

I was surprised and disappointed with some people in the army who treated their team members really badly. Sometimes this was done so a particular person could look good at the expense of someone else. Sometimes poor treatment was given out simply because someone was a bully. Interestingly, I met good and bad people across all ranks; there was no consistency in people of higher rank being better or more capable. Overall, though, I remember laughing a lot, and doing silly things with some really great friends.

Attending Business School, 2000-2002

In late 2000 I started a full-time Master's degree in Business Administration (MBA) at Manchester Business School, during which time I lived in Manchester.

I regularly visited Mum, and when I did not visit I phoned home weekly. She was often unwell and regularly got drunk and didn't eat properly. When I did visit her I had to manage her finances, ensure all the bills were paid and take care of her house. I was still providing some elements of care whilst studying a very demanding university course.

After Mum was sectioned in 1999, social services started to visit her to monitor her mental health. Some of the social workers were useless, whilst others were good. Several times between 2000 and 2002 Mum was admitted to the psychiatric care unit and these admissions varied from a couple of weeks to approximately two months. When she was there I was told that she was physically and verbally aggressive to staff, as well as demonstrating some very serious mentally ill behaviour. I did not know the full extent of this until I accessed Mum's medical notes years later.

Working for The Foreign and Commonwealth Office, 2003-2005

Keeping the Peace in Sudan

In 2003 I became a contractor with the UK Foreign and Commonwealth Office and was employed as a ceasefire monitor. My first contract was in the Nuba mountains area of central Sudan. I was part of an international team that was trying to maintain a ceasefire between the Sudanese government army and a rebel army. In addition, there were other armed groups in the area and sometimes these clashed with the government and rebel armies. I worked as an intelligence officer, a field monitor, a base commander and a liaison officer.

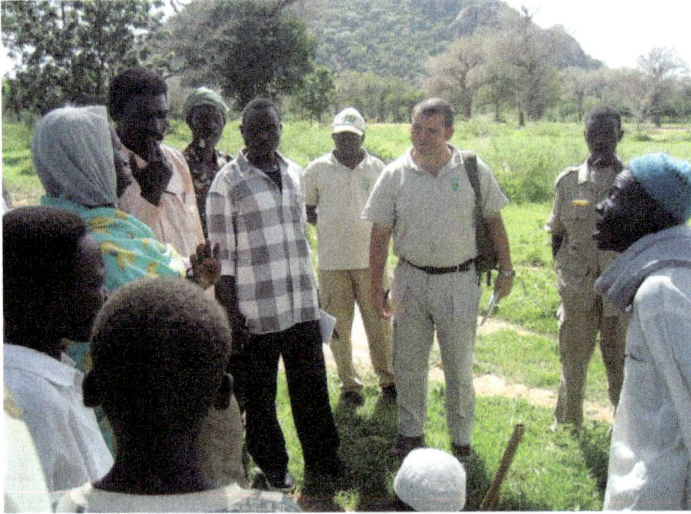

My experiences are too many for this book, but include:

- Working alongside organisations including the UN, Red Cross, Médicins Sans Frontières and various private contractors.
- Spending some time in Khartoum, the capital of Sudan.
- Spending three months in Northern Kenya liaising with charities and private contractors.
- Catching malaria and losing a lot of weight!

My boss on this assignment was a Norwegian General called Jan-Erik Wilhelmsen. He was focused, professional, realistic, inspirational and brilliant at managing teams. He had the ability to understand each of his team members and get the most out of each of them. To this day, he is the best leader I have ever worked for.

Visits home again involved solving lots of problems to do with Mum. One particular event involved meeting a financial advisor from a well-known building society who I will refer to as 'Fat Blob'. Fat Blob had taken a very persuasive approach to try to get Mum to move her savings into an investment scheme. I thought this investment was unsuitable for her, so I advised her not to go ahead, but then I had to go abroad again. Fat Blob then re-contacted Mum and persuaded her to move her money. Several years later this investment had massively gone down and Mum lost a lot of money. My view is that salespeople targeting vulnerable people is a form of abuse.

Monitoring a Border in Georgia

At the start of 2004 I left my contract in Sudan, and accepted a contract in Georgia, a country that had been part of Russia. I was employed as an international observer and was involved with monitoring the border between Georgia and an area called Chechnya.

One time when I came home on leave I went to visit my mother in Widnes. As I opened the door I heard her shouting for help and I found here face down in the hall, unable to move and very dehydrated. She said she had been there for two days. I gave some immediate first aid and then phoned for an ambulance. She had had a stroke, which means that part of the brain does not work properly. This badly affected the movement of the right side of her body. She spent several weeks in hospital and upon discharge had a very weak right arm and leg, but refused all offers of care packages. She refused to accept that she would struggle at home and often wouldn't talk to me about how she thought she would cope.

I briefly went back to Georgia, but then resigned because Mum was not coping at home. Whilst I was abroad she had several falls which resulted in hospital admissions because she repeatedly injured her head. I did not get a clear picture about what had happened, but neighbours told me she had often been drunk. I repeatedly tried to persuade her to move into sheltered accommodation but she refused, so I arranged for an emergency alarm system to be installed in her house so she could call for help if she had a problem.

Back to Sudan

In 2005 I spent seven months on a ceasefire monitoring mission in South Sudan, which in many ways was more difficult than my first time in Sudan. There was more conflict between the armed groups, with a lot of violence being committed by a government militia force that often targeted civilians. We dealt with some difficult situations, including shootings, sexual attacks and children being forcibly

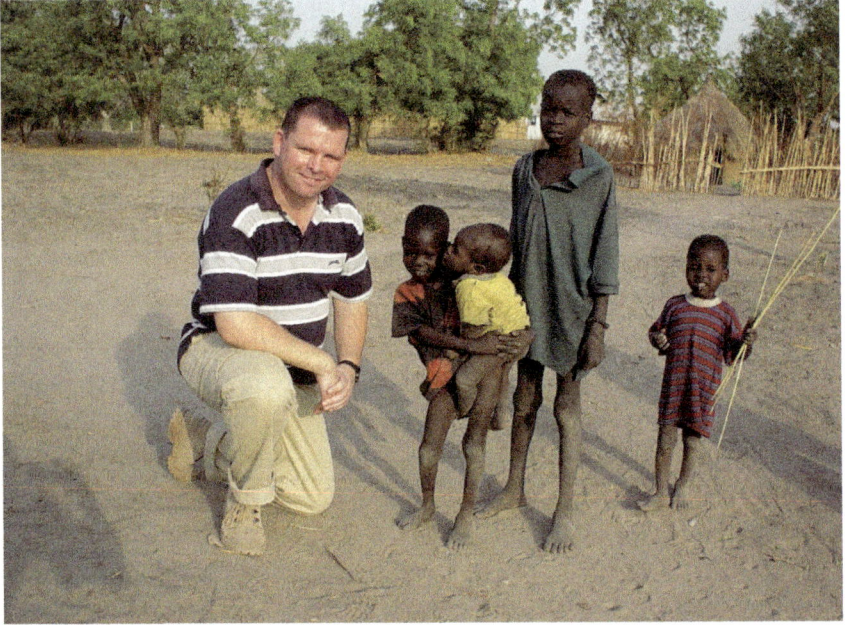

recruited as soldiers. I spent the majority of my time in a tented camp in South Sudan that we could only reach via a two-hour journey in a small plane from Northern Kenya.

Mum Being Targeted

When I was in Sudan in 2005 I was emailed by Trading Standards to say that Mum had been targeted by rogue builders who forcibly told her she needed a new roof. They had demanded that she pay them £4,000, which they had taken over two payments, one of £1,000 and one of £3,000. During this incident she had allowed these three men she didn't know into her house and also got into a van with them and allowed them to drive her to the bank.

By sheer luck I was coming home on leave, so I managed to get home before she gave them any more money. The scumbags phoned Mum the evening I got home to say they would need more money, and they would come to collect it the next day. I told the police what time they were coming, but the police said they couldn't have an officer in our house and that I would have to phone 999 when they arrived. I knew this wouldn't work, so I asked for help from two close friends from the army. One arrived that night and the other the following morning. Unfortunately, only one of these so-called builders came to the door because the others had apparently parked nearby. We easily detained him until the police arrived and he was arrested. When Mum realised that she had been conned she became very upset and depressed. I felt extremely angry that some people would sink so low as to exploit an obviously vulnerable elderly lady.

I had to return to Sudan, but the mission was due to close because the Sudanese peace deal was about to be signed. I decided to resign because I was concerned about leaving Mum. I had really enjoyed this contract and would have liked to stay until the mission closed, but I was worried that the rogue builders might come back.

Mum's Move To Sheltered Accommodation

When I got home I repeatedly suggested to Mum that she move into sheltered accommodation. Initially she refused, but after a lot of encouragement she finally reluctantly agreed. There was a new development being built in Widnes and we were able to get a one-bedroom flat. I delayed looking for a job so I could manage all aspects of the move, get her settled in her new flat, empty her old house and advertise it for sale. The new flat was part of a complex that had a warden and CCTV cameras on all entrances, so finally I had got Mum to a place where she was much safer.

Saudi Arabia and London, 2006

Mum settled into her sheltered accommodation flat and was finally safe. I was unemployed, keen to get a job and sending out numerous job applications. My mother's house was up for sale.

I was offered, and accepted, a short contract as a Security Consultant with an oil company in Saudi Arabia. When I was in Saudi Arabia I was phoned by the estate agent and told that someone had made an offer to buy the house, but the next week some idiots vandalised part of it and the potential buyer withdrew the offer. Unfortunately, I could not leave Saudi Arabia early. When I returned home I found that these idiots had trashed the garage. I could not believe that whilst I was taking time out of my life to try to help my mother, some fools were having mindless fun that was causing me massive problems.

Shortly afterwards I received job offers from the security company I had worked for in Saudi Arabia, the United Nations De-Mining department, and a logistics company based in the Middle East. I turned them down because I felt I could not work abroad again until I sold Mum's house. I then got a short project as a Security Consultant with a charity in London.

Later that year I finally sold the house at auction for less than it was worth. I had spent a lot of savings from my time working abroad because I had taken so much time off work. I had also turned down three jobs I would have enjoyed. Again I was sacrificing elements of my life to protect Mum.

Phone call with Halton Borough Council Social Services

A few months later, in late 2006, I received a phone call from a woman from Halton Borough Council Social Services. I remember the conversation as though it happened yesterday:

> 'Are you Valerie Raynor's son?'
> 'Yes, I am.'
> 'I am phoning to discuss her care,' the woman said.
> 'OK,' I replied.
> She then said, 'Right, I will send you a booklet about being a full-time carer and it explains about the carer's allowance.'
> 'Pardon,' I said, taken aback, 'did you say something about me becoming a full-time carer?'
> 'Yes, you are her next of kin and she needs help, so I will send the booklet about being a full-time carer. What is your address?'
> 'I think there has been a mistake here,' I said. 'At no point have I ever stated that I was going to become a full-time carer.'

'Does your mother need care?' she asked abruptly.

'Yes, she does, but I have not agreed to provide it,' I said.

'Am I right that she is a widow and you are her only child?'

'Yes,' I said.

'Right, well it is your responsibility so you are going to have to deal with it!' she said loudly.

'Excuse me, but I have my own life to lead,' I told her.

She then said, 'Oh I see, you are one of those sorts of relatives.'

'How dare you!' I said. 'You have no idea of what I have done for my mother over the years.'

'Really?' Her tone was sarcastic.

'Let me explain the situation to you,' I said. 'My father died when I was twelve years old ...'

At this point she interrupted me and said, 'Boo hoo for you.'

'What!' I shouted into the phone. 'How dare you speak to me like that! I have been a young carer since my father's death when I was twelve.'

'Well, you have had plenty of practice then,' she replied.

I then said, 'I want your name, and your boss's name and address.'

There was a long pause, after which she said, 'What do you want that for?'

'To write a letter about your conduct.'

'You are the one refusing to be a carer,' she said defensively.

I replied, 'There is no one on this planet who has the right to tell me to be a carer. What about my career ambitions? What about getting married and starting a family? How am I meant to do that on carer's allowance?'

'Not my problem,' she said.

I replied with, 'As I said before, what is your name, and your boss's name and address?'

She hung up the phone.

I was appalled that someone involved in organising care would speak to an ill person's relative like that. She knew nothing about Mum's history, my history or my present life. She thought she could just tell me to become a full-time carer and it would happen. Presumably me becoming a full-time carer would have made her life easier.

Working in the Nuclear Fuel Industry, 2007–2008

In 2007 I got a job as Head of Security for a company in the nuclear fuel industry, which involved managing security across sites in the UK, USA, France, Germany and the Netherlands. The company designed and made high-tech equipment called centrifuges that were used to make electricity, but could have been used to make bombs. Therefore the company was inspected by the governments of all the countries we operated in, and my job involved working with these governmental inspectors. I regularly travelled to the company sites in all five countries, as well as attending meetings with governmental officials in London, Washington, Paris, Bonn and The Hague. One of the highlights was giving a presentation at MI5 Headquarters regarding our security plans.

I used to visit Mum every two weeks to bring her shopping and manage her finances. She would do some shopping herself, but she would only buy bread, ham, and cheese. I used to buy her various ready meals and snacks, because she wouldn't cook a proper meal. I repeatedly suggested that I arrange a meals delivery service but she always refused. I did not know this at the time, but Mum was drinking excessively every day. Getting drunk would block out the voice she hears in her head.

In mid-2008 I met a young lady called Helen and we started dating. Little did I know that she would later become my wife and the mother to our daughter!

Bidding for Contracts and Getting Married, 2009–2012

In late 2008 I joined a consultancy company that provided advice on certain topics to other companies. I was given a project management role with a construction company, specifically helping them bid for contracts worth hundreds of millions of pounds to build new schools. I learned a huge amount about bidding for contracts. The best experience I had in this job was participating in negotiations that lasted several weeks, at the end of a massive bid for a contract worth £1.4 billion.

In late 2010 and early 2011 I did a nine-month assignment with a small company based in Liverpool. The company provided bid-writing services to other, mainly smaller, companies. The highlight of my time with this company was travelling to Latvia and giving a presentation on 'Bidding for Contracts' at an international business fair.

The personal highlight of 2011 was getting married to Helen! It was great to see so many friends in one place and I made a point of thanking people who had helped me throughout my life.

In late 2011 and early 2012, a friend and I ran a business supporting companies which were bidding for contracts. This was enjoyable, but unfortunately we made very little money. We decided to go our separate ways, and whilst it was shame things did not work out, I learned a huge amount about running a business.

Problems With Mum

I was still regularly visiting Mum to take her food and manage her finances, and Helen also kindly started to help. However, when we were not there all sorts of problems occurred.

One night in 2009 Mum was found in her night clothes lost outside the sheltered accommodation. She was found by two carers visiting another resident and they alerted the warden, who phoned me. I had to immediately stop what I was doing and drive to Mum's to persuade her to stay inside her flat.

Several times over the next few months she collapsed outside her flat and had to be helped home by strangers. I believe sometimes this was because she had been drinking too much alcohol.

In late 2009 she was admitted to hospital because the warden entered her flat one morning and found her collapsed when drunk. During routine checks in hospital an aneurism was found in her brain, which is a small blood clot that could dislodge at any time. If this small clot did dislodge it could kill Mum, but it was too risky to try to operate, so the aneurism was left.

In December 2009 Mum had another fall and was admitted to hospital. When she was due for discharge I raised concerns about her ability to care for herself. The doctor refused to admit her into any form of care unit and simply said that I would have to take her home with me. She was discharged on Christmas Eve and spent the next three nights with me in my flat. During this time she needed help to walk, help to take medication, and encouragement to eat, wash and to wear clean clothes.

After Christmas Helen and I took Mum to an NHS walk-in centre. The doctor initially tried to say it was my responsibility and I should take Mum home again. After a long, difficult discussion, the doctor eventually agreed to admitting Mum to a temporary care unit. During two weeks of proper care and medical supervision she put on weight, was steadier on her feet and said she was comfortable staying there. I said my mother needed to go into care, but her social worker refused.

Mum's situation worsened in January 2010, so social services arranged for four brief visits each day by carers. The carers helped by supervising her medication, but she refused any other help from them. Sometimes she would not give carers access to her flat.

In 2010 we noticed that Mum was wearing clothes covered in wee and poo. When I asked her about her soiled clothes she denied she had a problem, and said the clothes didn't need to be washed. Instead she had just hung items back in her wardrobe after wearing them. We also discovered that she had been incontinent in her bed, but was not changing the sheets and was sleeping in the wet and dirty bedding. Clearly, she was suffering with incontinence, so we bought some pads for her to wear. She initially refused to wear them because she said the voice in her head told her not to, but after a lot of encouragement she started wearing these pads. We also took responsibility for her laundry, including the items that were covered in wee and poo.

When unsupervised, Mum did not wash and often smelt of body odour. When I told her she needed to wash properly she initially said the voice in her head told her not to wash, so when we visited, Helen often helped her to have a shower.

Twice in 2011 Mum was admitted to hospital with breathlessness and difficulty with walking. Once she was discharged without my knowledge, but fortunately the warden at her sheltered accommodation informed me she had returned home, so I had to phone the care agency and arrange for the care visits to resume.

Twice in 2012 Mum was admitted to hospital with chest infections. Both times she had done nothing about her illness, and actions were only taken when Helen and I visited her. On both occasions Mum tried to refuse to go into hospital, but I insisted that she did. On one occasion she was again discharged without anyone telling me or the carers.

Starting My Own Business, 2012

In mid-2012 I decided to start my own business providing bid management and bid writing services. I bought a domain name and worked with a website designer to create a company website. Shortly after starting the business I got a big contract. It felt great to be completely in control of my work situation.

We were still visiting Mum at least every two weeks to provide various care, including taking her food, managing her finances, doing her laundry and helping her wash. The carer visits were ongoing but the carers were increasingly raising concerns about Mum's health. We could see that it was getting worse.

She was admitted to hospital once in 2012, following a fall when she was drunk. She was assessed in A&E and discharged the same day, all without my knowledge. Fortunately, one of her neighbours phoned and told me what had happened. I was working away from home, so Helen visited Mum and found her to be confused, still in the blood-stained clothes she had fallen in, and unable to eat or drink because her mouth was bleeding. Helen phoned the hospital and discovered that Mum had been given drugs to detox her system of alcohol and then sent home, but the hospital had not thought to tell anyone. Helen complained this was an unsafe discharge so Mum was readmitted to hospital immediately.

Mum's Admission Into Care, 2013

One freezing cold night in early January 2013 Mum collapsed into a bush near the entrance of her sheltered accommodation flat and was unable to get up for an hour. Fortunately, the warden returned at 10pm and found her. If the warden had not returned that evening, my mother would have frozen to death in the extremely cold weather.

During this fall she cut the inside of her right foot, so a District Nurse visited Mum to look at her foot. Helen and I visited her after the nurse's visit and saw her foot was badly infected and had not been dressed. The District Nurse had only placed a small plaster across the open, infected wound. We took her to a NHS Walk-In Centre and saw a nurse who said that the injury was now an ulcer which required a change of dressing every two days.

At the walk-in centre, for the first time ever, my mother admitted that she was not coping. Helen insisted on an emergency referral for respite care. After liaison with social services the decision was made that Mum would be placed into a care home for an emergency stay. When she saw her room in the care home, she smiled, stated that she liked it and felt like she was on holiday! We visited regularly during her emergency stay and she always said she was happy, was enjoying the food and the staff were very nice.

I was contacted by a really nice social worker about future care for Mum. I wrote a detailed explanation of everything that had happened, including how difficult things had been for me. Finally the decision was made that Mum would stay in the care home.

Life After Mum Went Into Care, 2013 Onwards

Since Mum went into care, both her life and mine have been vastly better. Mum is very happy and I have felt a massive sense of release. Her admission into care means that for the first time since I was twelve years old, someone else is caring for her. Twenty six years of me having to provide care have finally come to an end.

During the nine months after she went into care I had to send repeated letters to the Department for Work and Pensions to sort out Mum's pension. I only got a sensible reply when I threatened to inform the Commissioner of Pensions. Obviously there was no way my mother could have sorted this out herself, so I dread to think how many other elderly people are not receiving their correct pension.

Overall, though, life has been much easier and I have been able to concentrate on my personal life and my business. It was, and still is, a fantastic relief that I no longer receive phone calls saying Mum is in hospital, with an expectation that I would stop whatever I was doing and provide support.

Counselling, 2014

In 2014 I followed Helen's recommendation to undertake counselling regarding my father's suicide and my traumatic childhood. This was initially uncomfortable because I regard myself as a robust, self-sufficient individual. However the counselling sessions fortunately did not involve hugging trees, drawing pictures or getting in touch with my feminine side. They did, however, open up all sorts of stuff, encompassing many aspects of my childhood. My counsellor, Sharon, guided me through a journey of reflection, questioning pre-formed ideas and linking together various experiences.

The counselling has been a very beneficial experience, though at my core, I still remain a bit of a wierdo. I think I will always prefer the company of dogs to people!

Becoming A Father, 2015

On 13th July 2015, Helen gave birth to our daughter Beth. I was over-joyed at becoming a father!

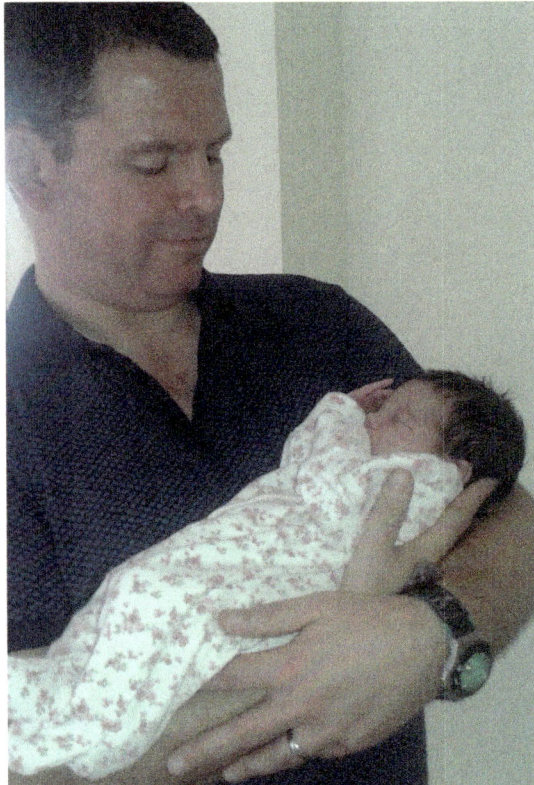

Common Factors Throughout My Adult Life

Below I describe some common factors that have applied through-out my adult life. These are important to understand because they influence some of the key advice in future chapters.

Involvement of Mum's Family

Unsurprisingly, throughout my adult life Mum's family did absolutely nothing to help her, even though I told them every time there was a problem.

They never visited Mum during the numerous times that she was in hospital or mental health units. They did not bother to see her follow-ing her stroke, after lots of falls or when she was sectioned. They did not visit her after she was targeted by burglars and rogue builders.

Usually Mum's sister and her husband visited her once or twice a year for approximately one hour. When they visited from Scotland they would combine their journey with a shopping trip, but they never took Mum shopping, took her out for a meal or even for a coffee.

During recent times Mum's sister did not visit her for four years between 2011 and 2015. In 2015 she visited her, which was the first time she had seen Mum's care home.

The attitude of my mum's sister and her husband has always been exactly the same as that of my grandparents: 'out of sight out of mind'. I find it disgusting that a family can abandon someone simply because they develop mental health problems.

Health & Social Care Professionals

Throughout my time as an adult providing care for Mum, I repeatedly met with health and social care professionals, such as social workers, mental health nurses, community matrons, incontinence nurses and psychiatrists. I often found these meetings very frustrating.

Many did mini-mental tests, which consisted of something like asking my mum to say the days of the week backwards or asking her date of birth. She would pass this test, after which the professional would say my mother had the mental capacity to make her own decisions.

I would point out that my mother regularly got extremely drunk, did not eat properly, did not take her medication correctly, could not manage her own finances, had been financially exploited in the past, had repeatedly put herself in physical danger and been helped by strangers, would not wash, and would wear clothes and sleep in sheets that were covered in wee and poo. The professionals replied by saying that she had mental capacity, so she could make these choices. I would also point out that she had no awareness that she was mentally ill and regarded it as perfectly normal that she heard a voice. The professionals stuck to their opinion and filled in their forms.

During this time I can only remember her having one mental health review when she had a brief appointment with a psychiatrist. I did not push for further appointments because the one appointment I attended was absolutely pointless.

It is important to note that Helen works in the NHS, has experience of working with people with mental illness and under-stands the processes within the NHS for patient care. Therefore she was able to provide me with a wealth of advice, liaise with health and social care professionals, and question some of their approaches. Without Helen's help it would have been even more difficult to deal with these people.

My Relationships With Women

It is worth describing my adult relationships with women, because these relationships have definitely been affected by my childhood.

During my adult life I have had four serious relationships with women. I have had other relationships but they are not for this book! My serious relationships are:

- A girlfriend when I was in the army.
- A girlfriend when I was a ceasefire monitor.
- A girlfriend when I was in the nuclear job.
- Helen, who I met in 2008 and married in 2011.

All of these women have commented that at times I can be unemotional, unaffectionate and self-sufficient, and they have all used the phrase "emotionally retarded". They have also said that I have a view on life that can be objective and unfeeling, as well as commenting that I am more affectionate with dogs than I am with humans!

It has taken my wife, Helen, an awful lot of effort and patience to chip away at my hard exterior. If it were not for her I would still be single and nowhere near as happy as I presently am.

CHAPTER FOUR
The Truth Is Uncovered

Letters Exchanged with Mum's Family

In 2014, following Mum's admission into a care home, I decided to investigate her condition and the treatment she had received. I sent letters to her family, asking them for any information they could give me about Mum's illness. A cousin replied, saying that Mum had been in Winwick Hospital, a psychiatric hospital near Warrington, in the 1960s. I had not known about this. My mum's sister and her daughter ignored my first letter, so I sent a second, after which I received a horrible reply from my aunt in which she tried to:

- Avoid explaining the history of Mum's mental illness.
- Blame my father for the actions he took with my mother.
- Criticise my father for committing suicide.
- Blame me for Mum and I staying in Scotland after my dad's death.
- Blame me for bruising Mum when I was restraining her.
- Avoid the fact that Mum's family had done nothing to support us.

I was amazed by the anger, lies and hatred in her letter. For years Mum's sister had done nothing to help, but now she had written a letter blaming everyone else and trying to avoid the truth. I wrote a detailed letter replying to every point she had made, telling her exactly what I thought of her and finishing all contact. It is obvious to me that the anger in the letter from my aunt was because she knew I was about to discover the truth. I was right.

I then wrote to Mum's GP in Widnes asking to access her medical notes, which I subsequently did. These pointed me to other hospitals which I also contacted asking for information.

Mum's Medical Notes

In spring 2014 I accessed Mum's medical records, which contained hundreds of pages of notes about her condition and the care she has received. A summary of those notes and other key information is as follows.

The first reference to my mother's illness is a doctor's note from 1961, which records a conversation with Mum's sister, when my aunt said Mum became mentally unwell at the age of 20–21. A doctor's note also dated 1961 says Mum is under the care of a psychiatrist in Winwick Hospital. Hospital discharge papers from 1963 say Mum spent six months in Winwick Hospital, during which time she received electroconvulsive therapy (ECT), which was a treatment for mentally ill patients involving electric shocks being given to the brain. In 1966 Mum is formally diagnosed as having schizophrenia and is prescribed anti-psychotic medication to suppress her symptoms.

My parents met and got married in 1970. They settled in Thingwall on the Wirral and I was born in November 1973. Mum's mental illness was again mentioned in 1974, months after my birth, when I was cared for by relatives from Dad's family.

We moved to Scotland in 1975 and there were notes from medical professionals near Oban. In 1980 there are numerous entries from the local doctor's surgery and a psychiatric hospital in Lochgilphead. Those entries all state that Mum was schizophrenic with affective disorder, which means she had mood swings. Later that year there were several entries saying the doctor had received letters from my father saying my mother was unwell and asking for help. In 1986 a doctor's note mentioned my father's suicide, but did not raise any concerns about Mum or I. A doctor's note from 1990 describes bruising I had left on Mum being raised as a concern by relatives. The same note describes Mum defecating in a bucket, emptying her poo into the kitchen sick, mashing her poo with her fingers and pushing it down the plug-hole. This entry is a statement of what happened but does not raise any concerns or make any suggestions.

In 1991 Mum moved to Widnes, so her medical notes contained entries from medical professionals in Widnes and the surrounding area.

I was amazed to discover Mum had mentioned to a doctor in 1995 that she was feeling suicidal. Her notes then said that in 1999 Mum had attempted suicide with a drug overdose, but it had not worked. I found it incredible that I had not been told this information. The medical notes continued by describing the time in 1999 when Mum was found at night wandering on a motorway, after which she was sectioned. There are two notable entries from the psychiatric unit which state "there was more than one occasion of hostility and verbal aggression towards staff", and "she was verbally threatening and staff believe she may become physically violent". Following Mum's discharge from the psychiatric unit in 2000 she was regularly visited by social workers. A note says "Health visitors have expressed concerns for their own safety because Valerie opens the door holding a screwdriver. Decision made that from now on staff will always visit in pairs" This was also new information to me. From 2000 onwards there were numerous entries describing Mum drinking too much alcohol and various hospital admissions.

Letters Exchanged with Dad's Family

In order to gain a balanced opinion of what had happened, I also wrote to Dad's family and asked them various questions. This brought some interesting information to light.

Dad's family said that prior to my birth there was no indication of Mum's mental health problems, though apparently she could be very quiet at times. As far as they were aware, the problems occurred after I was born.

I learned more about the times when Dad's family had looked after me when I was a baby. Apparently Mum's behaviour had been extremely erratic. She had not been providing adequate care for me, and she had been ignoring advice from medical professionals. She had been admitted to a psychiatric hospital, so some of Dad's family looked after me, which included increasing my food intake and providing affection. Apparently Dad asked Mum's family for help, but they refused, giving a variety of reasons why it would be inconvenient for them to look after me.

47

I also discovered more about Dad's decision to leave his sales job and move to Scotland to become a gardener. His sales job in England involved travel and sometimes he had to spend nights away from home. He was worried about Mum's ability to care for me when he was away, so he decided to find a job that would allow him to work close to our home. He also thought that moving to a quiet place would help Mum to relax, which was why he took the gardener's job offering a cottage as part of the job. Presumably this is also why Dad declined the job offer from his friend Bob, when I was about ten years old.

A Chat With Mum

As a final stage in my investigation, I decided to ask Mum about her attempted suicide. I visited her, had a relaxed chat about usual stuff, and then I quietly mentioned that I had found out. Mum obviously felt awkward, though she was able to tell me that in 1999 she had decided she was ready to die, so she had taken a lot of pills and lain down on her bed. She had expected to die, but when she woke up she realised the attempted suicide had not worked, so she decided to carry on with life. I asked her how she thought I would feel if she had committed suicide, but she avoided the question and started to become defensive. I decided not to push it any further.

A Final Word

I find it very sad that my dad has committed suicide and my mum has attempted suicide. I find the behaviour of some of my relatives to be absolutely disgusting.

I am extremely disappointed that Mum and Dad were not better supported by numerous health and care professionals.

I cannot change my past, but I do want to improve the future for young carers who are having difficult times. I also want to show that someone who has had a sad childhood can still have a happy adult life. The second part of my book gives advice for young carers across a range of topics.

CHAPTER FIVE
Lessons from My Experiences

In this chapter I mention some keys lessons from my experiences. I make observations regarding other people's opinions, people in authority, public sector workers, stress, and my emotions and behaviour. The two most important lessons I have learned are:

I Should Have Told Someone

As I mention in Chapter Two, My Experiences as a Young Carer, my biggest regret is that I did not tell my school friends or adults I trusted what my life was really like. I kept difficult parts of my life hidden, whilst I tried to have normal experiences in other parts of my life. However this did not address the key problems, and therefore nothing got better. If I could go back in time I would tell someone what was happening. I'm sure that good people would have helped both Mum and I.

Whilst I did not recognise it at the time, I think a lot of my approach to being a young carer was based on what I had seen my dad do. I had seen him make numerous sacrifices in order to provide care. I had watched him struggle alone but never demand support from others. I should have asked for help, even if Dad never did.

I Have Had to Work Hard to Achieve My Ambitions

It was clear that some people expected me to sacrifice my goals and become a full-time carer for my whole life, regardless of what I actually wanted to do. Achieving my ambitions, as a child and an adult, whilst also providing care for Mum has been challenging. It has taken a range of behaviours to achieve success, including hard work, carefully prioritising my time, questioning authority and sometimes breaking rules.

> **Key Advice and Quotes**
>
> Throughout the rest of the book, key advice appears in yellow highlighted boxes and quotes appear in orange highlighted boxes.

Other People's Opinions

Over the years many people have commented on my mother's condition and my actions as a carer. Some of those comments have been useful, whilst others were completely useless.

The following two tables summarise comments made by others, how their comments made me feel and the usefulness of their comments:

Sensible Comments

The sensible comments I received from other people are:

Comment From Others	How It Made Me Feel	Usefulness of Their Comment
"What you have done for your mother is incredible."	Proud, because someone had recognised my efforts and the sacrifices I had made in my own life.	Very useful – gave me encouragement to carry on.
"It is such a shame that you have come home on leave and now you will have to spend all your time sorting out your mother's problems."	Reassured, because someone else had recognised the impact of my mother's behaviour on my life.	Very useful – gave me encouragement to carry on.
"I think your mother would benefit from being in full time care, and it would relieve the pressure on you."	Incredible relief, almost to the point of crying, because my sole responsibility for my mother was coming to an end.	Incredible …

The sensible comments were useful to me because they gave encouragement and support. The people making those comments were genuinely trying to help and had taken the time and effort to try to understand the situation.

Stupid Comments

Unfortunately I have encountered lots of stupid people who formed opinions and made decisions without some or all the facts. Often they had no knowledge of my situation or the care I had already provided. Even though they had no experience or understanding of the situation, they still gave an opinion.

These are some of the stupid comments made by others:

Comment Made By Others	How Their Comments Made Me Feel	The Usefulness of Their Comment
"If she was my mother, I would do ...."	Angry, because it was a suggestion that I was doing something wrong.	None – the person making the comment had never provided care for a mentally ill parent.
"If she was my mother, I would provide any care she needed. I am surprised and disappointed you are complaining."	Angry, because it is a suggestion that I am being uncaring and selfish.	None – the person making the comment had never experienced the burden of providing care for a mentally ill parent.
"I would go to Social Services and demand they take responsibility."	Angry, because it was a suggestion that I had not liaised with social services.	None – the person making the comment had never dealt with social workers and community psychiatric nurses and did not understand the issue of Capacity.
"You need to have a strong word with your mother and tell her to stop drinking and eat properly."	Angry, because it is a suggestion that I had not attempted to change my mother's behaviour.	None – the person making the comment had no understanding of mental health behaviours.

Comment Made By Others	How Their Comments Made Me Feel	The Usefulness of Their Comment
"You are her Next of Kin so it is your responsibility."	Angry, because it seemed unfair that the burden of care was on me.	None – the person making the comment wanted to avoid having to do anything personally.
"I would not let her impact on my life, I would walk away."	Angry, because it was an unrealistic suggestion from someone who had never experienced parental illness.	None – the person making the comment had no relevant experience.

Often other people's opinions reflected what they wanted, for example, "It is your responsibility," or "You need to sort out this problem". Such people simply wanted to pass the problem to me and avoid taking any form of responsibility themselves.

Some people found it very easy to give criticism, but did not recognise that I was trying my best in awful circumstances. Sometimes there were no positive outcomes, just bad ones. Sometimes I had to identify the least worst option and work towards that, even though it was still a bad outcome that could be criticised.

There were other occasions when people gave opinions simply to make themselves sound important.

People's opinions are based on their life experiences, so people with limited life experiences have limited opinions.

People in Authority

I have been on the receiving end of a lot of behaviour and/or decisions from people in positions of authority. As a young carer, I was told what to do by adult relatives, and adults who were health and social care professionals. As an adult carer I asked for help and was refused by adults who were health and social care professionals. As an adult in various jobs, I have been told what to do by a range of bosses.

There are very clear comparisons between adults who spoke to me when I was a child, health and social care professionals who spoke to me when I was an adult, and bosses I have worked for who spoke to me when I was an employee. These are some of the sensible and stupid approaches I have experienced:

Sensible Approach

Some people in authority behave excellently. Earlier in the book I mention the Norwegian General I worked for in Sudan. Jan-Erik Wilhelmsen was firm, fair, and compassionate. He led by example, understood human relationships, accepted reality and planned for it, and always expected high standards.

The good people in authority asked open questions and valued my opinions. They wanted to understand the situation and act in the best way for all involved. They were realistic about the problems and likely outcomes, and they wanted to help and encourage me.

Stupid Approach

I have also seen many people in authority behave dreadfully. I have encountered people who made quick decisions without trying to understand the situation. Others have taken no account of the individuals in their team, or how to behave to get the best results from their team members. Some people in authority have gone as far as lying and cheating for their own personal gain, regardless of the consequences for everyone around them.

> *I have dealt with many people in authority. Some have been excellent and some have been dreadful. Don't assume that someone's opinions are correct, just because they are in a position of authority.*

Public Sector Workers

Some public sector workers (doctors, nurses, social workers, etc) have been excellent in providing help, whilst I feel I have been failed by many others. I have met a lot of public sector workers who were uninterested and unrealistic. Many of them filled in forms without actually doing anything, made judgements without knowing any facts, and repeatedly assumed I was willing and able to provide support without understanding anything about my life. In addition, a lot of them seemed to regard themselves as lone decision-makers, so there was no team approach to providing care for Mum and me.

I genuinely believe that the approach taken by many public sector workers put my mother at increased risk and put me under increased pressure.

I found that writing everything down helped in getting support from public sector workers. Keeping records makes it hard for people to ignore difficult situations.

> **Don't be afraid to disagree with public sector workers. Keep a record of things that happen and what is said in meetings.**

Stress

As a young carer I experienced extremely high levels of stress, and this continued during my time as an adult providing care.

Experiencing Stress as A Young Carer

I believe the reasons I experienced stress as a young carer include the following:

- I spent years trying to manage a situation that I did not want and I had not asked for.
- I was often coping with multiple stressful issues at the same time.
- Some aspects of my situation were out of my control.
- I was completely unsupported by family.
- I was making considerable sacrifices in my own life.
- I was expected to place caring responsibilities ahead of all aspects of my own life.

- I often received criticism for things that went wrong, rather than any sort of recognition or praise.
- I received criticism from people who occasionally visited, but left when things became difficult.
- I often felt that I was being exploited and unfairly treated.
- I felt that my needs were never considered by anyone.
- Sometimes, however hard I worked, it was difficult to make any progress.

Experiencing Stress As An Adult Carer

As an adult I have found providing care very stressful because it had a massive impact on my life. Sometimes things repeatedly went wrong despite my best efforts, such as the problems caused by Mum due to her inability to understand the situation. I also had to deal with uninterested professionals who offered no solutions, and I had to deal with the aftermath of cruel people exploiting Mum.

Why Is Being a Carer So Stressful?

I have worked in various jobs that might have appeared stressful, but actually they were nowhere near as stressful as being a carer. For example, working in Sudan involved some very difficult situations, but for a variety of reasons I experienced much less stress than when I was a carer. Ultimately, I had chosen to go to Sudan and I knew I could resign if I no longer wanted to stay. I was part of a team where everyone was working together to complete our tasks, the workload was allocated fairly and everyone supported each other. The workload was manageable because I would do periods of 10 to 12 weeks in Sudan and then have 2 to 3 weeks leave to travel elsewhere and relax. The final key reason why I did not find Sudan particularly stressful was that I and the team were having a positive effect on the ceasefire and we knew we were actually making progress.

I know friends and work colleagues who have said they are going through a frustrating time in their lives. However, that was often when they were doing something they wanted to do, but they had not been able to achieve absolutely everything.

I would suggest that carers are in a much worse position because they might be doing something they did not choose to do, might not receive any support and might feel they are not making any progress. Depending on the people in their lives, young carers might receive criticism and no praise, be expected to make unreasonable sacrifices, and to provide care over very long periods of time without any rest.

> **Being a carer can be very stressful. Anyone who tries to tell you otherwise is lying.**

My Emotions and Behaviour

I think it is useful to highlight some links between the behaviour of others, and my emotions and behaviour.

My Emotions and Behaviour as A Young Carer

I would summarise my emotions and behaviour as a young carer as follows:

- I felt let down by my family, health and social care professionals, and society in general.
- Sometimes I found it hard to dream about the future when dealing with the grim daily reality, which often seemed endless.
- I was unguided, angry and unsure of my own emotions. My attempts to express feelings were clumsy compared to my peer group, and any emotional vulnerabilities led to anger and withdrawal so I could not be hurt.
- I hid the truth and I focused on the areas of my life that were under my control. Other people would have seen behaviours like toughness and humour.
- I looked after my basic needs and either ignored or was unaware of my emotional needs. I became completely self-sufficient at a practical level.
- I was confident in some areas and I felt very comfortable making decisions.

- I was a natural problem solver and could analyse situations and suggest solutions without the need to follow procedures.
- I questioned authority and did not automatically accept what I was told by others in higher positions.
- It might have appeared that I was doing well, but under the surface I was not.

Negative Behaviours I Demonstrated

Sometimes stress has led to me demonstrate negative behaviours, both as a young carer and as an adult. I have made mistakes and sometimes I have treated others unfairly. There have been times in my life when I have felt consumed by anger. Sometimes I have encountered people who initially did something wrong, but I then responded far too severely.

The sequence of my emotions and negative behaviour normally went through the following eight steps:

Step	My Emotions and Behaviour
1	I felt that others were being selfish, unreasonable and inconsiderate.
2	I felt exploited and unfairly treated, which led to stress and anger.
3	The anger came out, which surprised other people.
4	The focus turned to my angry outburst, not the cause of the anger, even if my argument was valid.
5	The person I thought had done something wrong, was seen as the 'victim' of my anger.
6	I got a telling-off for being volatile and people thought I had a temper problem.
7	No one in authority tried to understand the background to the situation.
8	I became even more annoyed, angry and isolated.

I increasingly became dismissive of people in authority. I regarded them as stupid because they could not understand my situation, and I started breaking more of their rules because I did not respect them or their position. However, I was mistaken to assume that everyone in authority was wrong and consequently I made some decisions and broke some rules that I should not have done.

> **At tough times in my life I have been more likely to demonstrate negative behaviours. Those negative behaviours almost always made the situation worse.**

Behaviours That Led To Success

In my life, and my time as a carer, I have achieved many successes. All my successes were achieved by demonstrating positive behaviours such as determination, integrity, hard work, accepting set-backs and trying again. Positive behaviour towards others has resulted in successes in my personal life.

Key Lessons About My Behaviour

When I look back now I can see that my behaviour was hugely influenced by how others behaved towards me. Basically, when I did not receive love or consideration, I did not demonstrate love or consideration towards others. Later in life, when I did receive love, I demonstrated love towards others. This does not mean I can blame my behaviour on others, it simply allows me to understand my behaviour so I can control it.

I have had to accept that when I blamed others for the parts of my life that I was unhappy with, it did not improve the situation, even if I was right and they were to blame. I had to take responsibility for my own actions. I could not blame my actions on my tough childhood. Finally, I had to learn from the past, but move on with the future.

CHAPTER SIX
Advice on Certain Topics

This chapter offers advice to young carers. I have broken it into smaller sections to make information on different topics easy to find.

The topics and page numbers are as follows:

If I could speak to a younger me, this is what I would say:

Don't Measure Your Success Against Others

As a young carer you may feel that you are not succeeding in some parts of your life, so I want to give you my thoughts on success.

Let me say that providing care for someone else is an incredible achievement. I think you have succeeded as a person.

What Other People Might Say

Some people like to boast about aspects of their lives. At school some children may say things like, "I scored a goal on Saturday," or "I did really well in that test." Some will mention new clothes, games and belongings. A lot of adults also boast and say things like, "I get paid loads, I earn £XXX per year", or "I am buying a new car, it is a XXX". Boasting makes some people feel important.

Give Yourself Praise

As a young carer you might feel you are not doing well at some things, such as sport or exams. You might be unable to afford nice clothes or expensive belongings. These things might make you feel less confident. It can become easy to focus on what you are not good at, what you don't have, and where others seem in a better position than you.

Whatever others may say, I believe that success is living a life you enjoy and are proud of. I have met many people with lots of money and possessions who have:

- Led very dull lives.
- Led very lonely lives.
- Done nothing they are truly proud of.

You should be very proud of your achievements as a young carer, so rise above any petty nonsense, recognise how great you are and give yourself praise.

> *A life filled with silly social drama and gossip indicates that a person is disconnected from purpose and lacking meaningful goals. People on a path of purpose don't have time for drama. (Brendon Burchard)*

I recommend you create a one sentence statement that summarises your achievements as a young carer. You may decide to keep this to yourself or you may decide to say it to others. My statement is, "During my time as a young carer and adult carer I have provided excellent care for my mum." What is your statement? Write it in Chapter Eight – Tell Your Story. Say it to yourself. Remember it.

Take Responsibility for Your Life

Right now you are a young carer and it might feel like the world is on your shoulders. You might feel that you are always on the receiving end of other people's problems. You might also feel that you will not be able to achieve your dreams because you don't have the same opportunities as other people do.

You may hope that others realise how bad your situation is and offer help. However, many people cannot see things from someone else's point of view, so they will not understand your situation, even if the evidence is staring them in the face. If other people do not offer help you might feel sad, frustrated and angry.

The first step in improving your situation is taking responsibility for your life.

> **It is perfectly normal that at times you will feel sad and frustrated at your situation. However, if you always blame other people and feel self-pity, it is likely that nothing will get better.**

I know that you will have a variety of problems, some of which are out of your control, and that you feel you have few choices. However, you must remember that you still have control of many parts of your life. If you can take hold of these, and set goals for the future, then your situation will feel much better.

Understand the Situation

You need to understand the situation about the person receiving care. If you are considered old enough to provide care, you are old enough to be told.

Some adults might be reluctant to tell you the truth, believing that you are a child and therefore you should be sheltered from it. But if you do not know the truth there will be some things you are uncertain about, and these may lead to you feeling even higher levels of stress.

Examples of difficult topics and why you need to know about them are:

- If someone is dying, you need to know because this will allow you to prepare for the future.
- If someone has mental illness, you need to know because this will allow you to understand how they may react to things, and the difference between the person and their illness.

Some adults may try to make all the decisions themselves because you are a child. However, if you are providing care you should be treated with respect, involved in any family decisions, and your opinions should be taken seriously. It will be extremely stressful for you to be on the end of everyone else's opinions.

> *If you are providing care, then you are entitled to know what you are dealing with and be involved in decisions. You need to say this to the adults in your family. If an adult believes that the truth is too much for you, then you should not be involved in providing care.*

Learn From Your Previous Behaviour

Understanding Emotions and Behaviour

It is important to realise that many people are facing challenges that no one else knows about, and these challenges affect how they feel and how they behave. Everyone's behaviour is influenced by how happy they are, if their life is going well, and how other people behave towards them.

It may be that you have experienced tough times as a young carer and that has influenced your behaviour. You need to remember the following:

- Don't assume that people know about your situation, and even if they do know they may not use that knowledge to understand your behaviour. Many people will take your behaviour at face value.
- If people only see your anger, they will think you are a nasty person without ever knowing the difficulties you have as a young carer.
- If you act like you don't care about other people, those around you will assume that is true.
- People who have not experienced difficulties in their lives will not be as robust as you, so be gentle with them.

Because of the challenges you face as a young carer, there will have been times when you felt stressed and angry. These negative emotions may have resulted in you behaving in a bad way. You need to learn from these experiences.

Accept Mistakes You Have Made

In the stressful, demanding world of a young carer, it is certain that you will make mistakes. I have made plenty of mistakes, both as a child and as an adult. There are plenty of times when my behaviour has not been as good as it should have been.

However, it is important to remember that you are going through a very difficult experience and many other people could not do what you are doing. Therefore my advice is to go easy on yourself and put previous mistakes behind you. Learn from the experience.

If you're not making mistakes, then you're not doing anything. I'm positive that a doer makes mistakes. (John Wooden, US sports coach)

Some people may try to remind you of mistakes you have made. If people do this they are either trying to exert authority over you, distract attention from mistakes they have made themselves, or distract attention from something good you have done. Whatever their motive, I would suggest you simply ignore these people.

Limit How Much Time You Spend Reviewing the Past

It is important to learn from the past, but also to accept that there is no way of changing past events. Once you have identified the important lessons, you must try to move on with your life. If you have had to deal with idiots, learn from the experience, but then try to put them behind you. Focus on how good your life is, or will be, without them in it. If it helps, you could imagine putting them into a bin or flushing them down the toilet!

Unfortunately, some people never get over a previous traumatic event. They continually review what happened and feel the same negative emotions again and again. If they have personally made mistakes during an event they analyse what they did wrong and feel guilty. This means they continually feel emotions related to the past and don't enjoy what is positive in their life right now. Also, they don't dream about what they could do in the future.

As a young carer, planning for the future is a far better use of your time than continually reviewing past events.

Think About Your Needs

You have needs just like everyone else. You should not think that you have to sacrifice your needs because you are a young carer.

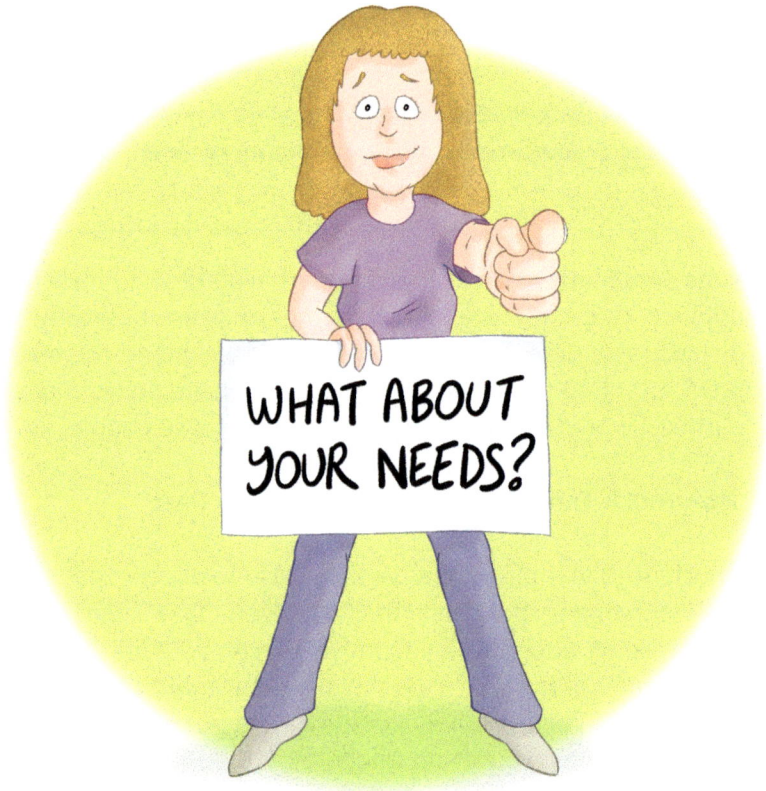

Some psychologists have tried to describe the needs of all human beings. Some ideas can be found on the internet and a common theory is called Maslow's Hierarchy of Needs. Maslow thought that all people had certain needs and that some were more important than others. He ordered them into a 'hierarchy', which meant that some were higher than others. His basic idea is a good one, and it is certainly something I can relate to from my experiences. Here is a loose version of Maslow's theory (and I hope he will forgive me for tinkering with it):

Physical Needs

Physical needs are the most basic needs for human survival. Physical needs include food, water, shelter, heat and clothing.

Safety Needs

Safety needs are the next level up from physical needs. Safety needs include feeling that you are physically safe and that your health is OK. This might also include financial security, such as having money, because that will affect your physical needs.

Love and Belonging Needs

Love and belonging needs arise because all people want to form relationships. Sometimes those relationships will be with family, sometimes with friends, and sometimes with loving partners such as girlfriends/boyfriends and wives/husbands. Most people will have a mixture of relationships with various people in their lives.

Esteem Needs

Esteem needs are the second highest need, according to Maslow. He stated that all people need to feel respected by others, as well as respect themselves. Maslow believed that people who did not feel respect from others, or did not feel respect for themselves, were in danger of suffering low levels of confidence and possibly depression.

Fulfilment Needs

Maslow called the highest need 'self-actualisation', but I think an easier word is 'fulfilment'. Maslow thought that once you had achieved all the other needs, you would feel completely fulfilled as a person. Different people will have different ideas about what fulfilment is, depending on their specific personal goals.

So What About Your Needs?

In your busy life as a young carer, have you ever stopped to think about your needs?

You might spend a lot of your time doing a range of caring tasks, such as feeding, washing or cleaning. It is likely that you will also offer emotional support such as love and reassurance.

Providing care might limit you from doing what you want and from achieving your potential. Therefore you may be sacrificing your esteem and fulfilment needs. If you are in a very difficult family situation you might not receive love, you might feel unsafe, or you might even be physically neglected.

Overall, you may feel that you have been failed by adults and people in authority. This could result in stress, anger and negative emotions, which are described later in this chapter.

> *As a young carer you may feel that many of your needs are not being met. Also you might not actually identify all your needs because you are used to making sacrifices and living under difficult circumstances.*

It is time for you to think about your needs. This is not selfish and can be done whilst continuing to provide care for someone else. As you read this chapter I want you to really think about what you need.

Set Personal Goals

Setting personal goals is crucial to staying positive about the future and feeling that things will get better. Setting goals will also help to identify what your needs are. I appreciate this is difficult to do when you are dealing with a range of immediate problems. You might be focused on issues like where the next meal is coming from, or how much money you have until the next social security benefits payment. It may also seem that you have to work very hard just to stop things from getting worse, and that actually you are not making any progress. However, planning for the future will help you to feel in control of your life.

> **Remember that you have as much right to achieve your goals as anyone else.**

Achieving some of your goals may take quite a bit of time. If this is the case, try setting yourself small daily targets. Setting a big target can seem too much and at times you may feel that you will never manage it. However, setting small targets will allow you to feel that you are making progress whilst you work towards your big goal.

Examples of Setting Goals

It may be that you would be happier if you were:

- Having more opportunities to make friends.
- Doing well at school so you could get a job you really want.
- Studying to get to college or university and study a subject that interests you.
- Playing sport.
- Having a break and being able to relax.

These are just examples and you may have completely different goals. In order to achieve your goals you may need help from other people. Examples of help you need could be money to pay for certain things, or assistance with providing care so that you have more time. These are things that other people such as your family and health and social care professionals can help with. The first steps are for you to identify what would make you happier and what help you need. I explain how to ask others for help in the 'Communicate With Others' section later in this chapter.

Decide Who You Listen To

Your situation as a young carer may be made tougher by comments from others. Some people may make fun of you or the person you care for. Some people may criticise what you are doing as a young carer, and others might try to tell you what to do. Some of these people may provide advice and encouragement but some may have no knowledge or experience of what you are dealing with. There is no definite guide for this, but you need to decide which people you are going to listen to.

Different Sorts of People

In order to understand comments that you may receive from other people, we first need to consider different types of people. My counsellor, Sharon, introduced me to descriptions of different personality types which have been really useful and allowed me to identify some of the personalities I have dealt with in the past. Here is a summary of these:

The Critic

- The basic need of the critic is Power.
- Critics set limits, enforce discipline, make rules and regulations about how life should be – they set the dos and don'ts.
- The critic seeks to criticise and find fault.
- They may also be assertive.
- The use words such as 'always', 'never', 'should', 'should not', 'must', 'ought to', 'have to', 'cannot' and 'bad'.
- They judge and criticise and use language such as 'because I said so', 'you are wrong', 'you have failed''.
- Their typical gestures include rolling their eyes in disgust, finger-pointing, folding arms and tapping feet in impatience.

The Kind Person

- The basic need of the kind person is caring.
- Kind people give advice, guide, protect, teach and sort out what makes sense and what does not.
- The kind person demonstrates warmth, support and love.
- They use words such as 'don't worry', 'good', 'can', 'positive' and 'choice'.
- They encourage and support and use language such as 'well done', 'you should feel proud', 'let me help you' and 'you are a good person'.
- Typical gestures include a consoling touch, head nodding, pat on the back and sympathetic eyes.

The Sensible Person

- The basic need of the sensible person is rationality.
- Sensible people work on facts, store memories, experience and feelings, and use those to make decisions.
- They use words such as 'situation', 'evidence', 'facts' and 'reality'.
- They make sensible suggestions and use language such as 'the situation is', 'our options are', 'this has worked in the past' and 'this has never worked'.
- Typical gestures include asking for opinions, listening, giving objective feedback, remaining calm, maintaining eye contact and making useful suggestions.

Comments from Kind and Sensible People

Hopefully you will have kind and sensible people in your life who demonstrate the behaviours listed above. In my experience, these people will seek to understand the facts of the situation, they will make realistic suggestions, and they will give credit and encouragement to those who are trying their best. Comments from these people will assist you in your role as a young carer.

Comments from Critics

Some young carers may have to deal with people who behave like the critic. These people will think they know better than everyone else. They may only see the situation from their point of view and give opinions without knowing all the facts.

Critics may also struggle to cope with bad news. They might criticise a young carer who tells them the news, interrupt or stop them, or dismiss their comments without trying to understand them.

> *If people are not helping, just giving criticism, and repeatedly saying that providing care is your responsibility, then I would suggest you stop listening to them.*

Understand People Who Try To Allocate Blame

Remember that the ill person is not to blame. There might be some situations where they are not helping themselves, but that may be because of a mental health issue. Ignore anyone who is trying to blame someone for their illness. People who try to blame others are simply being weak and dishonest. They are trying to avoid the problem and/or make themselves feel better by blaming others.

Ignore anyone who is trying to blame you for not providing enough care, or blaming you for any mistakes you may have made. If people have not been involved in providing care, they have not earned the right to an opinion. It is very easy to criticise others, but far more difficult to provide help and support. People who try to allocate blame are negative, so avoid them if you can. If you cannot avoid them, simply ignore what they say.

> *Successful people build each other up. They motivate, inspire and push each other. Unsuccessful people just hate, blame and complain (Unknown).*

Should Young Carers Listen to Adults?

The answer to that is, 'Maybe'. It depends on whether the adult is being kind, sensible or a critic.

This is a really serious point, because children are always told to listen to adults. However, when I was a young carer, many of the comments I received from medical professionals and family members were stupid. When I became an adult and I spoke with other adults about my mother, I again received stupid comments.

During recent times we have seen repeated instances of adults in positions of authority who have acted in terrible ways. We have seen police officers who have lied in statements, MPs who have cheated their expense claims, priests who have abused children and BBC directors who have ignored child abusers. None of these adults would have been any use to a young carer.

In my working life I have encountered other adults who were dishonest, unprofessional, selfish, self-motivated, unable to see somebody else's point of view, uncaring or simply stupid. In fact, I have witnessed adults behave in much worse ways than children.

I recommend that you listen to all comments, but then decide which ones are useful.

Communicate With Others

Communicating with others is crucial to improving your situation, so here is some key advice:

Remain Calm

When you do speak with other people about your situation you may feel all sorts of emotions. You may feel upset or even angry as you tell your story. Bear in mind that if you start criticising others for leaving you in this situation, they may become defensive. That may result in them trying to end the conversation, which is not what you want.

> **When you do speak with adults about your role as a carer, you must not get angry. You must state your case clearly and fairly.**

Describe Your Life As A Young Carer

Do not expect other people to understand your life as a young carer. Some people will not investigate or question how you live. Those that do see how you live may choose to ignore it or assume you are happy because you have not complained. Therefore, if you are not happy with your normal daily life, you need to tell people.

When you tell people you need to explain every detail of your life as a carer. Don't assume that people will link together pieces of information. Also, don't assume that people will remember what happened in the past and how it might relate to the present or future. If you have completed Chapter Eight – Tell Your Story, then you might want to read some passages out loud.

Express Your Emotions

Don't be afraid to express your emotions about being a carer. It is OK to say things like:

- I feel worried all the time.
- I feel lonely.
- My situation makes me angry.

Ask for Help

Don't be afraid to ask for help. If anyone accuses you of being selfish, it may be because they are trying to keep you quiet. It is fine for you to say:

- What about my childhood?
- What about my education?
- Why am I making all the sacrifices?
- Why is no one helping me?

Set Rules About Your Role

Try to set some rules about your role as a carer. Some possible questions to ask are:

- What are my responsibilities?
- What are other people's responsibilities?
- How are the caring tasks shared fairly?
- What support will I receive to perform caring tasks?
- What support will I receive to do activities that are important to me?
- Who will help if my caring role has a negative impact on my education?

Deal With Difficult People

If people ask questions, they should ask open questions, which allow you to explain your opinion. Examples of open questions are: 'What do you think?', and 'What do you suggest?'

You should watch out for closed questions, which only allow a yes or no answer; leading questions, which try to steer you to an outcome; and unreasonable questions, which give a one-sided opinion and try to undermine your opinion. Examples of these sorts of questions are: 'You are managing OK, aren't you?', 'I'm sure you agree with me about XXX?' and 'Do you really expect me to help looking after your mother?'

If adults ask questions that do not allow you to tell your story, I recommend you reply with: "Answering that specific question would not tell the whole story. Let me explain ..."

You may experience difficulties when trying to communicate with some people. It may be the case that the person:

- Has not understood the information you have given them.
- Understands, but thinks you are coping OK.
- Understands, but does nothing because of:
  o Laziness.
  o Not in their personal interests.
  o Believes there is nothing they can do.
  o Believes it is not their responsibility.
  o Simply does not care.

Some people might interrupt you, speak over you, tell you to "shhh", and say things like "stop complaining" or "stop whinging". Some health and social care professionals may try to ignore the problem. They might make a quick decision that you are doing OK based on something simple like school attendance or exam performance.

If this is the case, you either need to speak to the same person but communicate differently to make them take action, or speak to someone else.

If you do speak to the same person, you will have to take a firmer approach, but do not become angry. Some people only respond to a situation when it becomes personally important for them, but if you get angry they may try to stop the conversation.

> *Never argue with stupid people; they will drag you down to their level and then beat you with experience. (Mark Twain, US writer)*

Some suggested things you could say are:

- "I have explained that I am a young carer and that I cannot continue to provide all the care myself."
- "You have decided that it is acceptable to leave me in this awful situation, which is very disappointing."
- "If you continue to provide no help I will speak to a variety of doctors, nurses, teachers and social workers until I find someone who takes me seriously. I will tell them that I asked you for help and you refused."
- I know my rights according to the Children and Families Act 2014 and the Care Act 2014 (described in Chapter Seven). If you refuse to help I will approach charities to explain my situation and ask for support."

Identify Good Friends and Keep Them Close

Some friends will stick with you through good times and bad. They will understand how you feel and try to help you when things are tough.

You need to identify these friends and keep them close. My close friends have been very important to me throughout my life, and I wish I had told them about some of the difficulties I faced as a young carer.

Friendship is a two-way process, so you also need to look out for your friends. If they are going through bad times, you need to be there for them.

You will feel better if you talk to someone about your experiences as a young carer.

It's a good idea to tell these good friends about your role as a young carer. Even though they may not be able to assist your situation, simply chatting it through with someone will make you feel better. If you do not want to speak to your friends, you could phone some of the organisations listed in Chapter Nine such as Carers Trust or Childline.

You will probably have other friends who are there in good times, but don't want to help during bad times. These are often referred to as 'fair weather friends', because they are only with you when life is going well. You cannot rely on these people. Their unwillingness to help when you are in real need means they are not true friends. You may want to keep them in your life, but do not place too much importance on the friendship.

Manage Negative Emotions

Every person has times when they feel negative emotions. This can include feelings like stress, anger, sadness, frustration and loneliness. Experiencing these emotions is perfectly normal and is part of the brain processing feelings. I imagine that every young carer will experience some negative emotions. I don't think anyone can face the challenges you do and remain positive all the time.

Ignore Unhelpful Comments from Others

Some people will say they always have a positive outlook on life. They may even be critical of people who are experiencing negative emotions and say these people need to stop being negative. However, I have never met anyone who is able to take a positive approach to life all the time. I have known people who described themselves as positive, but then experienced one difficult thing in their lives and became upset.

> *It is easy to be positive when life is going well. However, when experiencing challenges for a long period of time, negative emotions are unavoidable.*

Do Not Feel Guilty

In amongst lots of other emotions, some young carers may actually experience times when they feel guilt. That may seem strange bearing in mind they provide care and support for someone else, but there may be times when they feel they could be better at some aspects of their caring role. There may also be times when they feel angry or resentful towards the person they care for, because caring has an impact on their life. Afterwards they might experience guilt because they had been angry.

If you are a young carer and you have experienced guilt, you need to remember that you have nothing to feel guilty about. Being a young carer is extremely tough and will result in a range of different emotions. Focus on all the good things that you have done, and remember guilt is just another normal emotion, along with many others.

Use Positive Thoughts To Counter Negative Thoughts

If you are a young carer and you experience any negative emotions, remember the following:

- Negative emotions come and go, so if you are having a low time, remember that it will not last forever and the emotions will pass.
- If you are experiencing negative feelings, you will benefit from encouragement and support. Try to spend time with people who understand your caring role and can provide that help.

- If people criticise you for being negative, listening to that criticism will make you feel worse, so try to ignore them.

There are some simple ways to train your mind to counteract negative thoughts with positive thoughts. One approach is:

- Identify something really positive that someone has said to you, or something really positive that you know you have done.
- Turn that into a positive memory.
- Whenever you have a negative thought, or you think of someone who has been nasty to you, remember your positive memory.
- The more you do this, the more the negative emotions will stop.

Another approach is as follows:

- Set a goal that you are working towards.
- Imagine what it would feel like to achieve that goal.
- Picture yourself as a winner, having got exactly what you want.
- Remember that feeling, hold onto it and remember it whenever life is tough.

Ask For Help

If you have negative emotions and they do not go away for a very long time, you need to ask for help. You may have developed depression and you might need help to beat it. Organisations you can approach for help are listed in Chapter Nine – Getting Support.

Manage Anger

Every person in the world experiences anger at some time. Young carers who are under a lot of pressure and are experiencing stress are very likely to feel angry. I certainly felt angry when I was a young carer and there were times as an adult carer when I have felt very angry indeed.

It is important that young carers should not criticise themselves if they feel angry. Anybody coping with your difficult situation would feel angry. What is important is having the ability to control the anger.

Emotions That Lead To Anger

Anger can be caused by lots of things, but generally people think about something, feel another emotion first, and then that emotion leads to anger. The emotions that can lead to anger include:

- Stress
- Anxiety
- Frustration
- Sadness

- Disappointment
- Shame
- Jealousy
- Guilt

Triggers, Thoughts, Feelings and Behaviours

In order to control anger we need to understand what happens in our bodies. There are some differences in opinion, but here is a simple model:

- There are things that make you feel angry which are called Triggers. These could include things that another person says or does, or being in certain situations.
- Once a Trigger happens, you will start to have Thoughts.
- As you concentrate on the Thoughts, you start to have Feelings, and your brain releases certain chemicals such as adrenaline.
- You might then take physical actions, so your Feelings lead to actual Behaviours.

The Behaviours are often negative, such as aggression, which can have very negative consequences. Other people will often only see the Behaviours, without understanding what you felt before your angry outburst. Therefore other people may assume that you are bad-tempered and/or violent, without understanding the background to your life.

Some people learn to control their anger, whilst others do not. People who do not learn to control their anger can find themselves in trouble and it can have a negative effect on their whole life. It is important that young carers learn to manage their anger.

Manage Your Anger

You need to create a strategy to deal with anger and ensure you don't bottle it up. People who have not experienced your challenges may suggest ways to manage anger which are unrealistic. You need to decide what is right for you.

If you have had angry outbursts in the past, you need to stop these. You need to focus on keeping calm in difficult situations, not letting others provoke you, and behaving in a winning way. Here is a suggested approach:

- Remember a time when you lost your temper and did something you regret.
- Remember how you felt afterwards.
- Remember the trouble you got into and what other people said.
- Focus on what you want to achieve in life.
- Imagine how that would feel.
- Take a deep breath.
- Focus on the fact that this immediate issue is not worth the hassle.
- Don't have another angry outburst.

Also, remember that if someone does a little thing that annoys you, don't take out all your pent-up frustrations on them. The person will be surprised at the anger in your reaction and you may be seen as the bad person. Try to keep things in perspective, take a deep breath, and remain in control.

It is essential that you find ways to relax and 'blow off steam' in a positive way. This is entirely your choice and could be an activity like listening to music, talking with friends, playing sport, doing exercise or doing a hobby. This will make you feel better both emotionally and physically. Crucially, it will help to lower your stress levels.

Deal With Bullies

Unfortunately, there are people in the world who take pleasure from causing distress to others. Whilst you might try to be nice to them, avoid them or ignore them; they will make efforts to find you and bully you. I don't have a magic solution regarding how to deal with bullies, but here are some thoughts.

Most bullies get a feeling of power from bullying, which makes them feel in control. The bullying can involve a range of activities, from something major to lots of small actions over a long period of time.

Therefore you need to ask the following questions:

- If you explained how you felt, would they stop or would they keep bullying you?

- If they like the effect they have on you, can you react differently to take away their power?
- If you told a sensible adult you were being bullied, could that adult make it stop?
- Can you accept their bullying until they are no longer in your life, for example, if you go into different classes at school or if they leave school?
- Can you beat them with words?
- Even if you win an immediate argument, will they keep coming back to you?
- If you hit them, can you win the fight?
- If you hit them, will it make you look bad?

Bear in mind that if you don't deal with bullies, they will continue to behave badly towards you. You may decide to stand up to a bully, but be aware that whilst that approach might stop the bullying, it might also make the bullying worse. Only you can make the decision regarding your approach.

I have stood up to many bullies, though sometimes this has caused me problems. However, it was very satisfying at the time!

> *Before you diagnose yourself with depression or low self-esteem, first make sure you are not, in fact, surrounded by assholes. (William Gibson, US writer)*

Limit Any Risk-Taking

It is perfectly normal to take risks and it is actually an important part of growing up and becoming an adult. Taking risks allows a child to explore their abilities, and having a good understanding of risk will help with future decisions as an adult.

Healthy risk-taking includes activities like sport, volunteer activities, travelling or entering competitions. These activities have the possibility of failure, but the consequences of losing are not serious.

Unhealthy risk-taking behaviour includes activities like playing truant from school, smoking, drinking excessive amounts of alcohol, stealing and unprotected sex. These activities have potentially very serious consequences, which could affect an individual's entire life.

As a young carer who is used to handling stress, you might feel able to cope with any risks and their consequences. Always remember, though, if things do go wrong, you might have to live with some serious consequences. If you are not happy with the possible consequences, don't take the risk.

Be Careful With Alcohol and Drugs

I appreciate that officially children should not experiment with alcohol and drugs, and therefore some people might say I should not include this section in a book for young carers. However, the reality is many children, both young carers and those who are not carers, will experiment with alcohol and drugs. Therefore I think it sensible to include this section.

The issues of alcohol and drug misuse are very complicated and I don't attempt to explain them in this book. I also appreciate that some young carers have parents or family members who are addicts, which will have a massive negative impact on the young carers' lives. If this is the case, and you are struggling to cope, I suggest you contact the organisations listed in Chapter Nine – Getting Support.

The advice I give is aimed at young carers who have taken, or are considering taking, alcohol or drugs. I also want to clarify that when I mention drugs in this section I am referring to recreational drugs like marijuana, cocaine and ecstasy. I am not referring to drugs that have been prescribed by a doctor for a medical problem.

What Alcohol and Recreational Drugs Do To People

I have never taken drugs, but I do drink alcohol. I know some of the effects are similar, so my advice applies to both alcohol and recreational drugs.

People behave very differently when they have taken alcohol and drugs. Many people lose their inhibitions and say things or do things they would not normally do. Whatever emotions they are feeling at the time, alcohol or drugs make them more intense, so:

- If someone is happy, alcohol and drugs will make them happier.
- If someone is sad, alcohol and drugs will make them sadder.
- If someone is angry, alcohol and drugs will make them angrier.

In the past I have occasionally got angry when I drank alcohol. Now I am older, more relaxed and much happier, I can use alcohol reasonably, but that has come with age and experience.

When Use Becomes An Addiction

When someone repeatedly uses alcohol and drugs, the body gets used to the chemicals and they have less of an effect. That person then needs to start increasing the amount of alcohol or drugs to get the same effect. Some people take so much alcohol and drugs that their body and mind craves it. People become addicted and start to focus on getting their next drink of alcohol or fix of drugs. When this happens people's lives tend to go very bad.

Addicts will often have problems at work and may lose their jobs. They may struggle with relationships and become, or stay, single. Many people who use alcohol and drugs excessively develop mental health problems. Some people might spend all their money on alcohol or drugs and lose their home. Whatever happens to each individual person, their life becomes a mess because of their addiction.

> *If you do experiment with alcohol and recreational drugs, be very careful not to take too much, or use them too often.*

Consider Any Experiences of Alcohol and Drugs

If you have experimented with alcohol and drugs, you need to be honest about how much you used and whether it was a positive experience. Did you do things you regret? Do you feel that you need the alcohol and drugs to cope with your situation? If you are starting to use too much alcohol and/or drugs you need to ask for help. Organisations you can approach are mentioned in Chapter Nine – Getting Support.

Cope With Bereavement

Some young carers will have to cope with the death of someone close to them. Some people die of old age, whereas others may die from other causes such as illness or an accident.

It is likely that immediately after someone passes away, you will feel numb and it may be difficult to accept that they are gone. Over time you may feel negative emotions such as anger that they have died, anger that perhaps doctors should have saved them, or guilt that perhaps you could have helped them more. These negative

feelings don't make you a bad person. It's perfectly normal to feel a range of emotions. You may also feel a great deal of sadness that results in you being upset and crying. Bereavement affects people in different ways and there is no right or wrong way to feel.

There is also no set amount of time that you will feel sad. However, after a period of grieving, you need to move on with your life. If you do not move on, you will remain feeling sad and upset.

Look After Your Physical Health

Many young carers will be very busy and therefore might struggle to complete all their tasks in the time available. This may result in eating food that does not take long to prepare, such as ready meals and snacks like crisps and chocolate. They may also find it difficult to find time for physical exercise. This can cause problems with physical health, such as gaining weight and not getting the right vitamins.

Eat Well and Exercise

Fruit and vegetables give your body energy and vitamins that are crucial. Chocolate, sweets, fizzy drinks and fast food might make you feel good when you eat them, but they are full of rubbish and you will feel hungry again very soon. Use them as a treat and limit how much you have.

Exercise is a crucial part of looking after yourself. It makes your body work better, is proven to reduce stress, and after exercise your brain releases chemicals that make you feel better. If you stay fit and healthy it helps your self-esteem.

> *Feeling good about your physical health will increase your confidence, reduce your stress and have a positive impact on many aspects of your life.*

Set Challenges

If you are not happy with your body, then change it. Take responsibility, set yourself a goal, create a plan and then do it. Maybe set a target for doing an event, like a 5km run, for a charity you care about.

Look After Your Mental Health

It is important that all young carers understand some basics regarding mental illness. Crucially, it is important to realise that having mental health problems is not a sign of weakness.

Some young carers will care for someone with a mental illness. Others will care for someone with a physical illness, but that person may experience mental health problems, such as depression, at certain times. All young carers may experience stress themselves, possibly at high levels, and therefore are at risk of developing mental health problems.

Types of Mental Health Problems

Some people have permanent mental health problems like bipolar disorder, chronic depression, schizophrenia or personality disorders. They might be on medication to reduce and/or control their symptoms.

Some people have temporary mental health problems like depression, anxiety or a nervous breakdown. Depression is when someone feels very sad for a long period of time and it affects their health. With the right help, people can completely recover from these.

Don't Be Afraid to Ask for Help

You must look after your own mental health. Look out for the symptoms of depression and anxiety, which are:

- Feelings of helplessness.
- Loss of interest in activities you used to enjoy.
- Appetite or weight changes.
- Difficulty sleeping.
- Anger or irritability.

If you are demonstrating any of the symptoms above you MUST ask for help. Do not suffer in silence, because that will make things worse.

Cope With Setbacks

Every successful person I know has had to cope with setbacks in their life.

People can experience setbacks in many different ways, such as failing to achieve a goal or breaking up with a partner. Sometimes you can do everything right and things still go wrong.

It may also be the case that you make mistakes. There may be times when you get things wrong, do things you regret, or say things you don't mean. You are only human, and all of us make mistakes.

Setbacks can make people feel sad, frustrated and disheartened. Focusing on the negative emotions will not improve your situation.

Go back to your goals, check they are still what you want to achieve, and then work towards them again. Communicate with people and do not be ashamed to say that you failed but you are trying again. Apologise for any mistakes, then identify how you will put things right.

The key to success, is to keep going.

Success is not final, failure is not fatal: it is the courage to continue that counts. (Winston Churchill, UK Prime Minister during World War Two)

Behave Like The Great Person You Are

An element of your life that is entirely under your control is how you behave towards other people. Many people may try to tell you how you should behave. However, they are not living your life, so their opinions may be rubbish.

Behave How You Would Like To Be Treated

If you want others to like you and treat you with respect, you need to behave like a nice person. If you want a boyfriend or a girlfriend, you also need to behave like a nice person. If you have angry outbursts, if you sometimes hit others, if you break rules, if you drink too much alcohol, etc, other people will just focus on that behaviour. This might result in others having a low opinion of you and avoiding you. This will make the situation worse because you may become further isolated.

Do not take out your frustrations on others. Most people will not understand the difficulties you face. Therefore if you take out your frustrations by being nasty to someone else, most people will think you are a nasty person. The focus will be your behaviour, not the underlying frustrations that you have because of your circumstances. Remember, picking on others is a tactic used by bullies.

Be considerate towards others, whilst also looking after yourself.

Avoid Peer Pressure

At school you might feel you have to do things because other children say so, which is known as peer pressure. My advice is, don't do anything you don't want to do. If people like and respect you they will not force you to do something you don't want to. If someone is trying to force you to do something, it is probably for their benefit and not yours.

Maintain A Sense of Humour

It is crucial that you try to maintain a sense of humour and, when possible, have fun. This will help you physically and mentally, and will reduce your stress. Maintaining a sense of humour will also help your relationships with others.

Be Confident and Competitive

You should be very proud of your role as a young carer and therefore you should feel confident in the type of person that you are. You should be competitive in life and want to succeed, not at the expense of others, but based on your own abilities. Do not try to measure your success against others; set your own goals and concentrate on achieving them.

> *You have the ability to achieve your dreams, so act like a winner.*

Remain Flexible

Sometimes aspects of our lives change due to something that we did not anticipate. Some people try to resist change; they want to live in the past, and they blame others for change. However, some change is unavoidable and the most successful approach is to accept change and respond to it positively.

> *It is not the strongest of the species that survive, nor the most intelligent, but the one most responsive to change. (Charles Darwin, UK scientist)*

Pursue Relationships

If some of my friends read this book and see that I am giving advice on romantic relationships, they will either laugh or cry! However, here are a few thoughts. When I was a young carer I stayed away from relationships with girls. Now I would take a completely different approach.

Being Attracted To Others Is Normal

It is perfectly normal, often when children become teenagers, that they find themselves attracted to others and want to start a relationship with them. This may be people of the opposite sex if they are heterosexual, or people of the same sex if they are homosexual.

Just because you are a young carer does not mean you cannot pursue a romantic relationship. If you really like someone, and you think the other person likes you, then tell them! Speaking to them may be nerve-racking, but it is well within your abilities.

Your Emotions May Change Over Time

When you are in a relationship you might stay with this person for a long time or you might break up after a while. Either is completely normal. As you get older you will probably be attracted to different people at different times. If you do start a relationship, the other person will probably be impressed that you are a young carer. You don't have to tell them everything about your caring role at first; you can wait until you both know each other better and then tell them slowly.

Unfortunately, during your relationships there will be times when you are upset, and you might experience heartbreak. There might be other times when you really like someone but they are not attracted to you. Those heart-breaking emotions always pass, however bad they might feel at the time. Relationships will make you both happy and sad, but overall they are very good and certainly worth the effort. Being with someone who cares about you will build your self-esteem and bring out the best in you.

Being in a relationship will have highs and lows, but overall, being in a relationship will make you much happier than staying alone.

Get An Education

There are a few people in life who pay no attention to education and qualifications and still succeed. However, they are rare and most of us need to pursue education and gain qualifications to achieve what we want. There are many benefits to gaining qualifications, such as:

- Improving self-esteem and gaining a sense of achievement.
- Earning money.
- Building a career.
- Allowing flexibility to change jobs.

It may not always feel like it, but school is actually the ideal time to study and gain qualifications.

Some adults find themselves stuck in jobs that they do not enjoy, but have to stay in that job because they do not feel qualified to change. Some adults may continue working whilst studying for qualifications in their spare time, but this can be difficult when they also have work and family commitments. Getting qualifications when you are at school is a much better approach.

Some people decide to pursue academic qualifications at school and/or university. Others may not like classroom studies and might struggle with written work. These people will probably be better suited to practical jobs where they use skills rather than doing lots of paperwork. Many schools and colleges offer practical courses, often linked to apprenticeships with employers.

Whichever route you intend to take, try to achieve a reasonable level of English and Maths. These skills will help in your personal as well as your working life.

Does Being a Young Carer Affect Your Education?

If you think that your role as a young carer is having a negative impact on your education, you must tell someone. If you sacrifice your education due to your caring role it will cause problems later in your life. You deserve to have an education and you should be allowed to pursue any qualifications you want.

> *Poor people cannot rely on the government to come to help you in times of need. You have to get your education. Then nobody can control your destiny. (Charles Barkley, US basketball player)*

CHAPTER SEVEN
Know Your Rights

If you are a young carer you may feel that you don't have any choices. You may feel that you have no option other than to provide care. However, you should be aware of some relevant laws. The two key points in these laws are that no child should have to provide care because there is no other choice, and no child should undertake inappropriate caring duties.

The various laws can seem complicated and therefore you may struggle to understand all your rights. If you would like some advice you can speak to the organisations listed in Chapter Nine – Getting Support.

The Responsibilities of Local Councils

Local councils are often referred to as local authorities, so that is what I will call them here.

Local authorities are responsible for ensuring that people who need care receive that care, and also that carers are being properly supported.

Therefore, you should never feel that you have to provide care, because actually it is the local authority's responsibility. You can decide whether or not you want to be a young carer, and if so, what care you should provide. This decision should be based on the type of care that is needed and the impact that providing care has on you.

Laws Introduced in 2014

Two laws regarding young carers were introduced in 2014. These are called the Children and Families Act, 2014 and the Care Act, 2014. These laws contain some key points for young carers:

Children and Families Act 2014

This Act states that local authorities must take reasonable steps to identify young carers within their area. When they have been identified, the local authority must assess if the young carers need support, and if so, what those needs are. This can be done via something called a Young Carers Needs Assessment, which is explained later in this chapter.

Care Act 2014

The Care Act 2014 requires local authorities to adopt a whole family approach. This means that when someone is receiving care, the local authority must look at the impact on everyone else in the house, including children. This act specifically states that if a family has a young carer, the local authority must consider if the young carer needs support. The act also states young carers should not provide inappropriate levels of care, and gives examples of inappropriate tasks.

Inappropriate Tasks for Young Carers

The law states that young carers should not perform some tasks that are performed by adult carers. It also states that young carers should not spend too much time caring for someone else because this can affect how they do at school, and whether or not they are able to do similar activities to other children or young people.

The guidance that goes with the Care Act 2014 states that "a young carer becomes vulnerable when their caring role risks impacting upon their emotional or physical wellbeing, or their prospects in education and life. This might include:

- Preventing the young carer from accessing education, for example, because the adult's needs for care and support result in regular absence from school or impacts upon their learning.
- Preventing the young carer from building relationships and friendships.
- Impacting upon any other aspect of the young carer's wellbeing."

There are various caring tasks which are regarded as inappropriate for carers under 18 years of age. Some examples are below:

- Personal care such as bathing and toileting.
- Difficult physical tasks such as lifting.
- Giving medication.
- Managing family finances.
- Offering emotional support to such a degree that the child is having to act like the parent.

If you are a young carer and you are performing any of these tasks then you must ask for help. The local authority is obliged to provide support to ensure you do not have to continue performing inappropriate tasks.

Local Authority Assessments

There are various assessments that local authorities perform to support young and adult carers. These assessments are not intended as checks on the care that the young or adult carer is providing, the assessments are to check what support carers need. Brief descriptions of these assessments are:

Young Carers Needs Assessment

A young carer's needs assessment is specifically for a carer who is under 18 years of age. The aim of this assessment is to check what duties a young carer performs, how the young carer is coping and if support is needed. This assessment takes place if:

- A young carer asks for an assessment.
- A young carer's parent asks for an assessment.
- The local authority thinks the young carer has needs (the young carer or their parent does not have to ask).

If you are a young carer, the young carer's needs assessment will assess several things. Firstly, it will assess if you actually want to be a young carer. If you do, the assessment will then look at the caring duties you perform and whether they are appropriate for a child. The assessment will also look at the impact that being a young carer has on your life, so it will look at things like the effect on your health, happiness, education, training, leisure opportunities and hopes for the future.

This assessment can take place with your parents and family present, or alternatively you can speak to a social worker in private. You have the right to ask for an adult to help present your opinions. This may be someone you know, such as a teacher or a family member. If you don't have an adult who can support you, then you can ask a social worker for an advocate. These are totally independent people who will help you through the process.

The person performing the assessment will also speak to your parents, and anyone else you or your parents want to be involved. If both you and your parents agree, the local authority may assess your needs and the needs of the person that is cared for at the same time. The assessment is also an opportunity to find out if you are eligible for any financial help.

All the people who are involved with the assessment will receive a written record of it. This will include whether the local authority thinks you need support and what will happen next. It will also explain what to do if you or your parents disagree with the assessment.

If your circumstances change, or the circumstances of other family members change, the local authority should carry out another assessment.

Transition Assessment

A transition assessment is different to a young carer's assessment. A transition assessment is for a young carer who is approaching 18 years of age, after which they will be an adult. There are different rights for young carers and adult carers, so the transition assessment looks at how the situation is changing and what the implications are for the young carer and the person being cared for.

The transition assessment will ask questions such as:

- Do you want to continue providing care once you become an adult, or do you want to stop providing care?
- If you do continue providing care, are you changing the tasks that you perform?
- What do you want to achieve in life, and if you continue to be a carer, what support do you need to achieve your goals?

If this is relevant to you, after the assessment the local authority will give you and your parents a report which summarises every-thing that was talked about and their recommendations regarding what should happen next. This will include any support necessary for the person being cared for, and support for you if you continue as a carer.

Carer's Assessment

A carer's assessment is available to anyone over the age of 18 who provides care for someone else. Therefore, if you have been a young carer, when you become 18 years of age you are entitled to have your situation reassessed. The assessment will consider how your caring role impacts on your education, employment and health. After the assessment, you will get a copy of the report that says what was discussed and whether any further support is recommended.

CHAPTER EIGHT
Tell Your Story

If you are a young carer and you are meeting people to discuss your role, I suggest you complete this chapter and take it with you. When I met medical and social care professionals and described Mum's care, I sometimes forgot some details that I wanted to say. To avoid this, I made notes before meeting people to ensure that I mentioned everything I wanted to. Having notes ready, and asking to read them out in a meeting, made it difficult for lazy adults to ignore the situation. It did not matter if the adult wanted to try to ignore the situation because I was ready to tell them the whole story.

Even if you do not plan to meet others, I believe you would benefit from completing this chapter. Many young carers are used to coping with their situation and do not realise all the difficulties they face. Therefore it would be a good idea to complete each of the following sections, which should help to make you fully appreciate the challenges you face and the sacrifices you make. You may decide to share the contents with other people or you may keep the details to yourself.

Your Statement of Praise To Yourself

In Chapter 6 I mention a statement of praise that I say to myself regarding my time as a carer. I suggest you write a statement relevant to yourself in the box below and remember it when times are difficult.

Describe Your Situation

Key Questions

Below is a table containing some key questions about your role as a young carer and spaces to write answers:

Question	Your Answer
Who do you care for?	
What caring tasks do you do?	

Question	Your Answer
Do you feel you receive support as a young carer?	
Does being a young carer have a negative effect on your personal life?	
Does being a young carer have a negative effect on your school life and ability to do homework?	
Does being a young carer upset you, for example, make you unhappy, stressed or angry?	
Does being a young carer have a negative effect on other parts of your health?	
Do you want to continue being a young carer?	
If you do want continue as a young carer, what support would you like?	

Your Normal Daily Life

At the start of Chapter Two – My Experiences of Being a Young Carer, I describe various aspects of my life as a young carer. You could use the description of my childhood as an example and then include some notes about your normal daily life under each of these headings:

Parents

Family

House

Money

Supervising Medication

Food

Transport

Neighbours

Social Life

Rule Setting

Your Experiences of Other People's Opinions

In Chapter Five – Lessons From My Experiences, I describe some of the comments that were made by other people, how those comments made me feel, and if the comments were useful. I have included a blank copy of the table below for you to include notes regarding comments other people have made to you.

Comment Made By Others	How Their Comments Made You Feel	Usefulness of Their Comment

Comment Made By Others	How Their Comments Made You Feel	Usefulness of Their Comment

What Would Help You?

If you want to continue as a young carer, there may be help that others can provide that would improve your circumstances. You must remember that it's not selfish to ask for help.

Below you could list some things that would help you. These are entirely your choice, but examples could be time when someone else provided care so you could pursue hobbies, spend time with friends, study, or simply have a break. List what you would like and why it would help in the table below:

I Would Like....	Why It Would Help

Other Notes

Use the space below to make any other notes that you feel are useful.

CHAPTER NINE
Getting Support

Being a young carer is extremely tough and there is no reason for you to try to manage alone. You deserve support and there are various people and organisations you can approach to get help.

I have made some suggestions regarding the order that you speak to people, but you may decide to do things differently, depending on the difficulties associated with your situation.

Regardless of what support you get from anyone else, it's good to chat about your caring role with your friends. Talking through your challenges with people you trust will reduce your feelings of being alone. Your friends will provide emotional support, even if that is simply listening to you chat about your experiences.

Speaking to Your Family

If you have a good relationship with your family, then these are the first people you should speak to. Some family members may not know about your role as a young carer, or if they do, they may not fully understand the difficulties you face. You could complete Chapter Eight – Tell Your Story before you speak to them so that you prepare everything you want to say. Hopefully they will listen to you and offer support. However, if they try to avoid the problem, or say it is your responsibility, I suggest you look elsewhere for support.

Speaking to Teachers

Some schools now have a formal policy which states how they can support young carers, but even schools that don't have a formal policy will be aware of the issue. If you feel that your role as a young carer is affecting your school life, then you should speak to a teacher that you trust. You could also speak to a teacher if you have not received support from family and you are unsure how to get help. Again, it will probably help if you complete Chapter Eight – Tell Your Story before you speak to them.

Organisations to Approach

There are various organisations you can approach for help and support. Some of these are charities, whilst others are part of the National Health Service (NHS). Each of these organisations has considerable experience in advising and supporting young carers. The details of these organisations are:

Carers Trust

Carers Trust works to improve support, services and recognition for anyone living with the challenges of caring, unpaid, for a family member or friend who is ill, frail, disabled or has mental health or addiction problems. They do this with a UK-wide network of quality assured independent partners, through unique online services and through the provision of grants to help carers get the extra help they need to live their own lives.

With locally based Network Partners, they are able to support carers in their homes through the provision of replacement care, and in the community with information, advice, emotional support, hands on practical help and access to much-needed breaks. They offer specialist services for carers of people of all ages and conditions, and a range of individually tailored support and group activities. A description of their activities with young carers can be seen at the following webpage: https://www.carers.org/what-young-carer. This webpage allows users to search for carer activities in their area, and gives contact details for those local projects. Alternatively, to find your nearest Network Partner, call 0844 800 4361.

Carers Trust runs **Babble**, which is an online community where young carers can find others in a similar position, chat, have fun, share experiences and access information and online support from an expert team. Babble is supervised by a team of qualified youth, community and social workers, who are on hand to provide expert advice in a friendly, safe environment. They provide support via chats, posts, confidential email or Q&A. The webpage for Babble is: https://babble.carers.org/.

Carers Trust also runs **Matter** which is for carers aged 16–25 and was developed after research into the specific needs of this age group around issues such as gaining independence, leaving home, finding employment and opportunities for higher education. The webpage for Matter is: https://matter.carers.org/.

Carers UK

Carers UK gives expert advice, information and support, connects carers so no one has to care alone, and campaigns for lasting change. To get information and advice on caring, visit www.carersuk.org, phone the Carers UK Adviceline: 0808 808 7777 (Monday to Friday, 10am-4pm) or email: advice@carersuk.org.

The Children's Society

The Children's Society is a national charity that runs local projects, helping children and young people who are at their most vulnerable. The Children's Society provides support for young carers across the UK and runs a programme called **Include**, which is specifically for young carers. The website is: http://www.childrenssociety.org.uk/what-we-do/helping-children/young-carers.

NHS Choices

NHS Choices is an NHS run service that provides advice across many areas. They have a general webpage for all carers, which is: http://www.nhs.uk/conditions/social-care-and-support-guide/Pages/what-is-social-care.aspx

NHS Choices also has a specific webpage for young carers which explains the rights of young carers, allows users to search for carer activities in their area, and provides contact details for local projects. This website is: http://www.nhs.uk/Conditions/social-care-and-support-guide/Pages/young-carers-rights.aspx

NHS Choices runs a free telephone service called **Carers Direct** which provides advice to both adult and young carers. The phone number for Carers Direct is: 0300 1231053.

NSPCC (National Society for the Prevention of Cruelty to Children)

The NSPCC is a children's charity in the UK, specialising in child protection and dedicated to the fight for every childhood. They work to safeguard children at risk of abuse and neglect. The NSPCC website is: www.nspcc.org.uk

The NSPCC runs a free telephone service called **Childline** which allows children to speak to a counsellor regarding any problems they have, including challenges they might face as a young carer.

The Childline website is: https://www.childline.org.uk/info-advice/.

The Childline phone number is: 0800 1111

Samaritans

Samaritans is a charity that offers support to people who are struggling to cope, round the clock, every day. People can phone their helpline and talk to a volunteer about any challenges that may be upsetting them. The Samaritans volunteer will listen and support them to talk sensitively through their options and explore their feelings. If specialist help is needed, Samaritans can direct the caller to other sources of support.

The Samaritans website is: www.samaritans.org which gives details of local branches.

The Samaritans helpline number is: 116123

People can text Samaritans for support on: 07725 909090 or email at: jo@samaritans.org

Local Authorities

In Chapter Seven – Know Your Rights I mentioned that local councils (who are often called local authorities) are responsible for ensuring that people who need care are receiving care, and that carers are being supported. You could try approaching your local authority directly, but it can be difficult to find the right person to speak to. Therefore I suggest you first speak with your family, teachers and/or organisations listed above, so they can help communicate with local authorities. When you do communicate with a local authority, you can request one of the assessments that are described in Chapter Seven – Know Your Rights.

CHAPTER TEN
Conclusion

Despite a difficult childhood and challenges in my adult life, I have lived, and am still living, a very interesting and enjoyable life.

I have no doubt that I developed some very useful skills during my time as a young carer, skills which have assisted me in later life to achieve my ambitions. Even though parts of being a young carer were extremely tough, there have been some positive outcomes.

> *I've never met a strong person with an easy past. (Unknown)*

If I can manage to succeed in life, then so can you. I hope this book helps you along the way.

Best wishes,
Mike

REFERENCES

Data/Research

Material Referenced
The UK Census 2011 stated there are over 177,000 young carers in England and Wales.
The BBC, with assistance from The Princess Royal Trust for Carers, conducted a survey ("Kids Who Care" 2010) in Surrey. They surveyed 4,029 pupils in ten secondary schools and found 337 had caring responsibilities. This indicates there could be 700,000 young carers across the UK.
A quarter of young carers said they were bullied at school because of their caring role. Carers Trust, 2013.
Young carers are more likely than the national average to not be in education, employment or training (NEET) between 16 and 19. The Children's Society, 2013.
Young carers achieve much lower GCSE exam results than average, the difference between nine B's and nine C's. The Children's Society, 2013.
Various entries in Valerie Raynor's medical notes, held at Peel House Lane Surgery, Widnes, Cheshire.

Quotes

Material Referenced
"A life filled with silly social drama and gossip indicates that a person is disconnected from purpose and lacking meaningful goals. People on a path of purpose don't have time for drama." Brendon Burchard.
"If you're not making mistakes, then you're not doing anything. I'm positive that a doer makes mistakes." John Wooden.
"Success is not final, failure is not fatal; it is the courage to continue that counts." Winston Churchill.
"I've never met a strong person with an easy past." Unknown.
"It is not the strongest of the species that survive, nor the most intelligent, but the one most responsive to change." Charles Darwin.

Material Referenced
"Successful people build each other up. They motivate, inspire and push each other. Unsuccessful people just hate, blame and complain." Unknown.
"Before you diagnose yourself with depression of low self-esteem, first make sure you are not, in fact, surrounded by assholes." William Gibson.
"Never argue with stupid people, they will drag you down to their level and then beat you with experience." Mark Twain.
"Poor people cannot rely on the government to come to help you in times of need. You have to get an education. Then nobody can control your destiny." Charles Barkley.

Published Material

Material Referenced
Maslow's 'Hierarchy of Needs', Wikipedia
Berne, Eric, *Transactional Analysis in Psychotherapy*, Grove Press, 1961.

Laws

Material Referenced
Care Act 2014
Children and Families Act 2014

Charity Details

Material Referenced
Carers Trust, emails, 2015
Carers UK, letters and emails, 2015 and 2016
The Children's Society, letters and phone calls, 2015 and 2016
NHS Choices, emails, 2015 and 2016
NSPCC (National Society for the Prevention of Cruelty to Children), letters and emails, 2015
Samaritans, letters and emails, 2015 and 2016